To my mother

MASTERING
the Art of
SELLING

A GUIDE TO BUILDING A SALES CAREER IN THE
FMCG INDUSTRY

MANAL HADDAD

DISCLAIMER

While the author has made the utmost effort to ensure the written content's accuracy, the author cannot be held responsible for any personal or commercial damage caused by misinterpretation of the information contained herein.

The advice mentioned in this book is not a substitute for any professional advice from established professional leaders and consultants in the field.

The book is intended for informational purposes only and should be treated as such. You should not make any financial decisions based solely on the content of this book without consulting an expert.

CONTENTS

ABOUT THE BOOK

"Sales is the most important aspect of a company, which in turn is about how well you treat your customers and stay ahead of your customer's requirements." – Mark Cuban

The naïve ones among us believe sales is all about selling. While this might be true a decade ago, it certainly does not apply to today's world. Sales has witnessed a dramatic evolution in the past 25 years. The days of aggressive selling to customers are long gone. Today, it is all about building strong relationships and effective communication. If you want to succeed in sales, you need to focus on creating a connection with your customers and understanding their needs and preferences.

This book is a game-changer for anyone looking to develop a career in sales. It covers all the essential information you need, from the skills required to excel as a sales manager to the effective use of business analytics. With this book, you will be equipped with the knowledge and confidence to succeed in the competitive world of sales.

CHAPTER 1

THE TRUE DEFINITION OF SALES

If you aim to excel in your chosen field, it is imperative to have a deep understanding of its basics. The foundation of any profession is crucial, as it sets the stage for your future success. Irrespective of your chosen field, you will always have to start from scratch. Therefore, to thrive in your profession, you must begin by mastering its fundamentals.

The best way to start learning about something is through definitions. Since you aim to build a sales career, let us begin with its definition. There is no single definition of "sales." Numerous authors define the exact term differently. For instance, the Merriam-Webster dictionary defines sales as operations and activities involved in promoting and selling goods or services. Other authors define sales as all the activities undertaken to sell a product or service to a business or a consumer. While both these definitions are correct, they do not encapsulate the true value of sales in today's business.

In the current day and age, sales is all about helping your prospects solve their problems. It is the process of paying attention to people's needs and pains and assisting them with their problems. Similarly, selling is about understanding the needs of prospects by actively listening to them and then creating a plan to help them fulfill their needs.

WHAT ENCOMPASSES SALES

Here is a list of activities that come under sales.

1. Following Up – The sales department plays a crucial role in proactively pursuing and following up with potential leads, ensuring no opportunity goes unnoticed.

2. Building Lasting Relationships – The era of the "hard sell" is long gone. In the present age, it is no longer enough to simply persuade a customer to purchase your product or service. Building a lasting and trustworthy relationship between the company and the buyer is the hallmark of modern-day sales.

3. Closing – Effective closing refers to turning prospective customers into actual customers. This can be achieved not only through personal meetings marked with firm handshakes but also through phone calls or online communication. With the right approach and communication skills, effective closing can be accomplished successfully, regardless of the medium used.

4. Retaining Customers – Ensuring customer satisfaction is paramount to retaining customers. By prioritizing customer happiness and making sure they are satisfied with the product or service, you can instill confidence and trust in your brand.

Assume you are a sales professional in the office equipment industry. It is crucial to be knowledgeable about your products and services. When a customer contacts you looking for printer paper, do not just try to sell them the most profitable option. Instead, ask them about their specific needs, such as the type of printer they use and how quickly their office goes through paper. This information will help you recommend the best paper options, including high-quality materials if necessary. With this approach, you can be confident that you are providing the best solution for your customer's requirements.

Once you have made the sale, reaching out to the customer for feedback is crucial. Even if their experience was negative, assure them that you are committed to delivering exceptional service in the future. By doing so, you can establish a robust and long-lasting relationship with the customer and retain their business for years to come.

IMPORTANCE OF SALES IN A BUSINESS

To achieve success in any business, the sales department plays a critical role by bridging the gap between a company's offerings and its customers. However, establishing a successful sales career takes more than just selling. A skilled salesperson must build long-lasting relationships with clients, ensuring their complete satisfaction with the product or service provided.

SALES IS ABOUT CARING

Sales is all about caring for your customers and providing them with the best solution to their problems at the right time. It encompasses a wide range of activities and tasks that are aimed at delivering the best value to your customers. By focusing on your customers' needs and providing the best solutions, you can build trust and loyalty that will help you achieve success in your sales efforts. Ultimately, the true definition of sales is about being confident in your ability to provide exceptional value to your customers every time.

CHAPTER 2

WHAT MAKES SALES DIFFERENT FROM MARKETING

B oosting revenue and increasing the company's bottom line are the ultimate objectives of both sales and marketing. Although many people think that sales and marketing are interchangeable, they are two distinct functions that are deeply intertwined. While small organizations may have the same staff members performing both sales and marketing functions, as companies grow, these roles and responsibilities become more specialized, highlighting the vast differences between sales and marketing.

A marketing team plays a crucial role in paving the way for the sales functions. The team's primary responsibility is to inform and attract potential customers and leads towards your business and the products/services it offers. On the other hand, the sales team works directly with the prospects to convert them into loyal customers.

MARKETING VS. SALES

Sales can be defined as a transaction where a seller offers tangible or intangible goods or services to a buyer in exchange for money. On the other hand, marketing encompasses a comprehensive range of business activities aimed at creating, communicating, and delivering value to clients, customers, and partners.

Marketing teams are experts in promoting, pricing and distributing products and services to meet the needs and wants of their valued customers. Meanwhile, sales teams are specialists in achieving target sales and fulfilling sales volume objectives.

The scope of marketing and sales functions differ significantly. While marketing involves advertising, market research, public relations, and customer service, all of which contribute to a better understanding of customer needs and the development of targeted offers, the sales team focuses on persuading customers that the product/service meets their requirements and convincing them to make a purchase. This distinction highlights the importance of both functions in driving business growth and success.

DIFFERENCE BETWEEN MARKETING AND SALES GOALS

Promoting the company's products and services is the cornerstone of our marketing strategy. A marketing department is responsible for pricing products in a way that appeals to customers and keeps the company competitive in the market. Additionally, they ensure that customers are well-informed about how the products can fulfill their wants and needs. With long-term marketing goals in mind, marketing campaigns span over several months, allowing the creation of an effective and impactful marketing plan.

Sales employees are driven by the goal of achieving their assigned quotas and fulfilling their targets. These goals are typically short-term and measured on a monthly basis. The sales management team and department heads set specific targets for each salesperson to meet their goals. With a clear understanding of what is expected of them, sales employees are confident in their ability to succeed.

MARKETING STRATEGIES AND SALES STRATEGIES

As the scope and objectives of these two functions vary significantly, the strategies employed also differ significantly. A marketing strategy primarily focuses on creating product or service awareness amongst the relevant audience. Therefore, it is crucial to have measurable marketing strategies to evaluate their effectiveness in achieving the desired outcomes. A few examples of such strategies include:

- Digital, TV, or print advertising
- Social media
- Public relations
- Brand marketing
- Relationship marketing
- Direct mail
- Viral marketing
- Email or cold calling

Sales is all about convincing your target audience to buy from your business; thus, it involves a great deal of interpersonal interaction. The key objectives of a marketing strategy are to develop a strong sales force, employ effective conversion methods and techniques, stand out amongst similar businesses in the market, and closely monitor and analyze sales performance. To accomplish these goals, your sales strategy must be well-structured and meticulously planned, taking into account all the key factors that can impact your business's sales. Your sales strategy can include the following:

- Cold calls or warm calls
- Face-to-face meetings

- Networking
- Trade fairs or promotional events
- Direct sales
- Abandoned cart emails.

ALIGNING MARKETING AND SALES STRATEGIES

For your organization to achieve its goals, it is imperative to have a well-aligned sales and marketing strategy. Any misalignment between them can result in a waste of valuable resources, time, and money. In addition, it can lead to a failure in converting potential customers into actual customers, which can cause a significant decrease in the Return on Investment of your marketing and sales efforts. Research has proven that a lack of alignment between the sales and marketing departments can reduce a company's revenue by 10 percent or more. Therefore, ensuring that your sales and marketing strategies are in perfect harmony is essential, which will undoubtedly lead to increased revenue and profits for your business.

Coordinating sales and marketing efforts can bring about tremendous benefits to a business. It can significantly increase the customer retention ratio by up to 36% and boost sales win rates by almost 40%. But the most remarkable advantage is the whopping 208% increase in revenue from marketing activities. It is a proven strategy that businesses should not overlook if they want to achieve remarkable growth and success.

HOW TO ALIGN SALES AND MARKETING

As a sales professional, it is vital to establish effective communication channels between the sales and marketing departments.

By ensuring that the sales team has a say in creating marketing tools, you can align the activities of both departments toward a common goal.

CHAPTER 3

UNDERSTANDING
THE SALES FUNNEL

Mapping out the sales process is crucial for any business to convert potential customers into paying ones. A sales funnel, also called a revenue funnel, helps visualize a customer's journey before purchasing. The funnel analogy is apt because it represents the large number of potential customers at the top and the smaller number that makes it to the bottom by completing the purchase. By understanding this process, businesses can take steps to optimize their sales funnel and improve their conversion rates.

As a seasoned marketer, I can confidently say that a prospective customer's journey from the moment they learn about your business to when they finally make a purchase can be complex. However, with a well-designed sales funnel, you can guide them through this journey, ensuring they remain engaged and committed to purchasing. By understanding the different stages of the funnel and tailoring your approach to meet the needs of each prospective customer, you can increase the chances of converting them into loyal customers. This is why online and offline businesses rely on sales funnels to guide their sales activities and drive growth.

IMPORTANCE OF A SALES FUNNEL

If you are an experienced sales professional looking to make crucial decisions in your sales career, the sales funnel can be an incredibly powerful tool. With its help:

1. You can predict and quantify the value of sales in the future.

2. You can provide a clear and effective process for closing more deals.

3. You can generate statistics on the number and size of deals needed to meet or exceed targets and make informed decisions to help you achieve your goals.

4. You can explain to your sales team how to move prospective customers through a smooth process and close deals. This will lead to maximized sales force productivity and increased conversion rates.

UNDERSTANDING THE SALES FUNNEL

To ensure the success of your business, it Is crucial to have a clear understanding of your business's vision, target market, and marketing strategy before diving into developing your sales funnel. For example, if you plan to launch an online cosmetics store, following specific steps will be necessary to achieve success. A confident approach and solid plan allow you to easily navigate the process and achieve your desired results.

Designing your sales funnel can allow you to customize it to your needs. However, the four key sales funnel stages are tried and true and can provide a solid foundation for any sales strategy. It Is important to remember that with these stages, you can guide your potential customers through the sales process and convert them into happy customers. The typical four key stages of the sales funnel are:

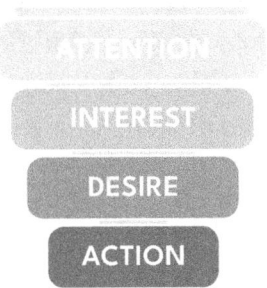

1. Attention/Awareness

2. Interest

3. Desire

4. Action

STAGE 1 - ATTENTION/AWARENESS

At the initial stage of the sales funnel, you have the opportunity to educate your potential customers about the unique value proposition of your product, service, or solution. This is the perfect time to showcase how your offering can effectively solve their problems and help them achieve their goals. Doing so can instill confidence in your prospects and set the foundation for a successful business relationship.

Prospective customers often reach this stage after discovering your website through a social media post, an ad, a Google search, or other means. At this point, they have already shown interest in your product or service, and it is up to you to showcase your value proposition and convert them into loyal customers.

STAGE 2 - INTEREST

Here, your potential customers are actively searching for a product, service, or solution to meet their needs and solve their problems. This presents a unique opportunity for you to capture their attention with engaging content and showcase the value of your offerings. With a confident approach, you can effectively communicate how your solutions can provide the best results and help your customers achieve their goals. So, do not miss out on this chance to establish a strong connection with your audience and demonstrate your expertise in your industry.

STAGE 3 - DESIRE

When your prospective customer reaches the third stage of the funnel, they are at the crucial point of deciding whether or not to buy from you. At this stage, your product or service details, pricing, and other factors play a vital role in influencing their final purchase decision. Rest assured, by clearly understanding your product's unique features and competitive pricing, you can guide them toward making a purchase.

At this stage, you unleash the power of your sales techniques, leveraging sales calls, webinars, sales pages, and other effective methods to close deals and win over potential customers.

STAGE 4 – ACTION

Congratulations! In the action stage, your potential customer is ready to seal the deal and become your customer.

UNDERSTANDING THE IMPLICATIONS OF THE SALES FUNNEL

Sales personnel who want to build a successful career need to do more than just have knowledge about the sales funnel. They must know how to use the sales funnel to their advantage with confidence.

Understanding sales funnel leakage is crucial for any business. It refers to the number of people not progressing from one stage of the funnel to the next. Although sales funnel leaks are common, excessive leaks can indicate underlying problems in your sales operations that must be addressed. Identifying and rectifying these issues can optimize your sales funnel and boost your overall sales performance.

TOP OF THE FUNNEL

If you are experiencing leaks at the top of your sales funnel, it is a clear sign that your prospects are losing interest faster than they should. In such a scenario, assessing whether you are targeting the right type of potential customers is crucial. It is essential to keep in mind that investing your sales efforts in prospects who do not align with your product or service's target audience is simply a waste of your valuable time and resources.

Moreover, to effectively guide your prospective customers toward conversion, you must prioritize creating compelling emails, irresistible CTAs, captivating landing pages, and engaging website content.

MIDDLE OF THE FUNNEL

You might be wondering why you are unable to move your leads into the latter part of the funnel, even though you are getting the right ones. The most likely reason is that you are failing to stay in touch with them. Fortunately, there is a solution to this problem - investing in a reliable Customer Relationship Management (CRM)[1] tool. Doing so lets you take control of your leads and build strong relationships with them, ultimately leading to more conversions and increased revenue.

You should never forget that a significant 60% of potential customers will purchase either from you or your competitors. Therefore, engaging them effectively and maintaining their interest in your product is crucial, or they may switch to a competitor's product. Confidence in your product and strategy is vital to retaining customers and growing your business.

---

1 https://www.businessnewsdaily.com/7839-best-crm-software.html

With an integrated CRM tool, you can track prospective customers' activity and automatically follow up with them. This will guarantee that your product or services stay at the forefront of their minds, increasing your chances of attracting and converting them into loyal customers.

BOTTOM OF THE FUNNEL

You may be experiencing leaks from the bottom of the funnel because you are not targeting the right prospective customers. By identifying and pursuing the most valuable and profitable leads, you can ensure you are not letting any potential customers slip away. With a targeted approach, you can convert more leads into loyal customers and increase your bottom line.

When faced with such a situation, it is crucial to implement a Lead Scoring process[2] to gain valuable insights on which leads to prioritize and respond to promptly. This approach will help you stay ahead of the competition and maximize your sales opportunities.

2 https://pipeline.zoominfo.com/marketing/lead-scoring

CHAPTER 4

THE FOUR PILLARS OF SUCCESSFUL SALES

Whether you plan to launch your own FMCG venture or aim to secure a position at a top FMCG corporation, you need a solid understanding of the four fundamental pillars of sales. These pillars, which include Sales Operations, Sales Process, Sales Coaching, and Sales Training, are the key to unlocking the full potential of your sales team.

Now, let's delve into each of these pillars in detail.

SALES OPERATIONS

Sales operations are the bread and butter of a successful sales team. As a sales employee, you will tackle daily tasks, such as logging calls, filling out forms, scheduling, attending weekly meetings, and exceeding your sales quotas and objectives.

In the sales department, the sales operations pillar plays a crucial role in providing a solid foundation for the sales team to excel in their responsibilities. With a well-structured sales operations system, the sales team can function at their highest potential without any hindrances or obstacles. This enables them to focus solely on their primary task of selling, leading to increased productivity and better results. Moreover, as you advance in your career, the sales operations pillar will equip you with the necessary data to track and evaluate the performance of each individual in your sales team, providing valuable insights into their strengths and weaknesses.

With a well-structured sales operation, you and your sales team can stay focused on generating sales instead of getting weighed down by paperwork and endless meetings. Streamlining your processes can boost your performance and help you achieve your sales targets with greater confidence.

SALES PROCESS

The sales process is a well-defined approach that sales teams use to close a sales deal effectively. A well-crafted sales process provides each sales employee with a clear and specific path, leaving enough room for improvisation, ultimately leading to successful sales closures.

It all starts from the moment they lay eyes on a list of potential customers and ends with a definitive decision of either a win or a loss. Nowadays, numerous companies have sales processes that extend beyond the point of sale closure. This primarily entails providing impeccable aftersales services to both existing and new customers.

With a clearly defined sales process, your sales team can efficiently acquire as many prospective customers as possible. Without one, you risk hindering your team's objectives, leading to unproductive steps and individualized sales processes. You can guide your team toward success by implementing a robust sales process.

SALES COACHING

As a sales manager in an FMCG company, you are responsible for coaching your sales team and ensuring their success. This involves closely monitoring the performance of each employee and providing regular feedback to help them improve. By mentoring your sales team, you can guide and support those struggling to meet their objectives. As a sales coach, you have the confidence and expertise to lead your team to success.

A top-notch sales coach will have an in-depth understanding of the performance metrics of their sales team acquired through the sales operation. They will leverage this data to pinpoint areas of improvement and implement effective solutions to boost team performance. Additionally, they will generously acknowledge employees who achieve outstanding results and address under-performing team members, ensuring that the team maintains a high level of excellence.

SALES TRAINING

Sales professionals at every level, whether seasoned industry veterans or fresh-faced rookies, must embrace continuous learning to achieve excellent results consistently. As a sales training manager, you are responsible for implementing an effective sales training plan that equips your team with the latest and greatest selling tools and techniques. With the right approach, you can instill confidence in your sales team and help them reach new heights of success.

It is essential to understand that sales is a constantly evolving field where the trends and techniques keep changing at a rapid pace. Therefore, to build a successful career in sales, you need to stay on top of these changes and adapt to new ways of delivering value to the customer. Using the same old script or presentation repeatedly can lead to poor results. Instead, it is crucial to encourage your sales team to innovate and develop fresh approaches to meet the customers' evolving needs. Doing so ensures your team stays ahead of the game and achieves the desired results.

A meticulously planned sales training program covers all the essential factors and empowers your team with the necessary knowledge tailored to their individual learning styles. On the other hand, an ill-conceived sales training plan wastes your team's time and can leave them confused and unmotivated. By investing in a well-designed sales training plan, you can be assured that your team will be equipped with the skills needed to excel and succeed in their roles.

CHAPTER 5

IMPORTANCE OF
SALES OPERATIONS

B ased on the discussion in the previous chapter, it is clear that sales operation is the backbone of any sales team. It encompasses all the essential tasks, processes, and activities that enable, drive, and support the frontline sales representatives to sell more effectively.

With the help of engagement techniques, software tools, and training, a skilled sales operations leader empowers their team members to concentrate solely on achieving business results.

By leveraging data-driven strategies, cutting-edge technology, and best practices, sales operations structure the selling process to achieve maximum success. With a focus on training, they boost the probability of closing deals and guide the sales team towards unprecedented levels of achievement.

It is impossible to overstate the importance of sales operations in today's leading sales organizations, as it significantly impacts sales productivity, performance, and efficiency. Here are some compelling reasons that underscore the critical role played by sales operations.

1. IT ALLOWS THE SALES TEAM TO SPEND MORE TIME ON SELLING

Based on research, it has been found that sales representatives typically devote only one-third of their total work time to selling. Given the high cost of hiring sales representatives, they must focus their efforts on selling. If they are not doing so, it means that they are spending their valuable time on other activities, which ultimately results in a waste of money.

However, sales operations are an effective way to streamline and organize the sales process, enabling your sales representatives to focus on what they do best - selling. By taking care of the time-consuming clerical work, sales operations allow your team to pursue and close deals, ultimately driving business growth and success.

2. IT HELPS YOU IDENTIFY UNDER-PERFORMING EMPLOYEES

In a well-structured sales team, it is common to find that 20% of the employees fit perfectly in their roles and deliver excellent results. However, the bottom 20% of the sales team comprises employees not suited for the position. Unfortunately, no support, guidance, education, training, or incentives can help these candidates improve their performance. In such cases, removing them from the team is the optimal decision. Doing so ensures the team comprises the best performers to drive the organization toward success.

With an efficient sales operations department, you can pinpoint underperforming employees and take corrective action to ensure that your entire sales team consistently delivers top-notch results.

KEY TAKEAWAY

Investing in sales operations is a crucial step toward boosting a company's revenue and improving the customer experience. A well-equipped sales department, powered by the latest technologies, can significantly enhance productivity and efficiency. Therefore, leveraging sales operations is the key to achieving business success and staying ahead of the competition.

CHAPTER 6

DEVELOPING A SALES OPERATIONS STRATEGY

With a clear understanding of the significance of sales operations, developing a top-notch sales operation strategy is crucial.

As you embark on your sales career, you may find yourself in the position of a sales operation specialist with considerable technicality. Alongside conducting data analysis and carrying out basic sales platform analysis, having a sales operation strategy in place can set you apart and increase your opportunities for promotion. With this in mind, it is essential to develop the confidence and skills needed to strategize effectively and contribute to the growth of your team.

You must follow these six proven steps to develop a winning sales operation strategy.

STEP 1 – IDENTIFY YOUR MAIN OBJECTIVE

A sales operation team plays a pivotal role in ensuring that every sales representative in your team has all the necessary tools, resources, and processes at their disposal to make successful sales. With this objective in mind, all the activities carried out by the sales operation team are focused on maximizing sales and achieving optimal results.

As a sales strategy developer, it is crucial to have confidence in your abilities to meet sales objectives. You may need to adjust your current strategy by evaluating and discarding time-consuming and pointless tasks to achieve this. This approach will help you create a more efficient sales operation strategy, improving your chances of achieving your sales goals.

STEP 2 – ALIGN MARKETING AND SALES DEPARTMENT

Effective collaboration and communication between the marketing and sales departments are crucial for any FMCG company's success. As a sales team member, you need to lead by example and ensure that your team works closely with the marketing department to achieve the company's goals. While it is expected to face coordination issues, you must take charge and ensure that your team works in harmony with the marketing department to achieve maximum results.

Thus, your next step should be to enhance coordination between the two departments. This can be easily achieved by leveraging technology to simplify the process. For example, using contract lifecycle management platforms can significantly enhance efficiency by reducing negotiation time and helping you achieve your goals.

STEP 3 – STREAMLINE THE PROCESS OF ACCESSING CONTENT

As a sales team member, your time is one of your most valuable assets. That is why it is crucial to develop a sales operation strategy that identifies time-saving procedures, tools, and workflows. Doing so can maximize your productivity and achieve greater success in your sales efforts.

The primary focus should be content, which is critical in engaging prospective employees. Sales operations can make a significant impact by taking charge of the task of arranging and maintaining a centralized repository of content. By doing so, sales reps can easily access the information they need, making them more confident when communicating with potential candidates.

STEP 4 – FACILITATE THE PROCESS OF QUALIFYING LEADS

Creating a sales operating strategy is a crucial step toward achieving business success. To ensure that the sales reps' time and energy are spent effectively, it is vital to facilitate the process of qualified leads. By doing so, the sales team can focus on closing deals with a higher probability of success. This improves the overall efficiency of the sales process and positively impacts the company's revenue and profits.

Therefore, when crafting a sales operation strategy, it is essential to devise a process to assess and rank leads based on specific parameters. By funneling only the most lucrative leads through the sales pipeline, your sales team can expedite the deal-closing process and bring in more revenue with greater ease.

STEP 5 – INTRODUCE CRM

To optimize your sales team's efforts, it is imperative to implement and maintain CRM tools, systems, and technologies with complete accuracy of data entry. Additionally, embracing time-saving techniques like automation of repetitive tasks is equally important. These steps will help you streamline your sales processes and boost your team's productivity.

STEP 6 – IMPLEMENTING AN INCENTIVE PLAN

As the leader of your sales operation team, you are responsible for hiring and onboarding the best sales representatives. However, before you proceed, it is essential to determine the appropriate compensation plan that reflects the value of their time and effort. To accomplish this, you can leverage the data available from your company and other FMCG industries situated in your country, allowing you to determine the ideal compensation plan for your high-performing sales team.

With the right base salary and sales commission percentage structure[3] in place, you can significantly enhance the performance of your sales team. Designing a structure that incentivizes your sales reps to make the right kind of sale instead of just any sale is crucial. Rest assured that taking the time to create a well-designed compensation plan will pay off in the long run.

KEY TAKEAWAY

Always keep in mind that the sales operations strategy you develop will ultimately lead your sales team to reach their full potential. By creating and implementing a sales operations strategy that follows the steps mentioned above, you can ensure that your sales reps perform at their best and that your company will generate more revenue and improve its bottom line.

---

3 https://blog.close.com/sales-commission-structure-for-startups

CHAPTER 7

IMPLEMENTING THE BEST SALES OPERATIONS PRACTICES

You probably would have picked up some of the best sales operations practices from the previous chapter. And now, get ready to dive even deeper into some of the essential practices needed to maintain a high-performing sales operations team.

1 – RECRUIT DATA-DRIVEN PEOPLE

To excel in sales operations, data analysis is crucial. Hence, recruiting individuals with exceptional critical thinking skills who can efficiently analyze data is imperative. If your team members struggle with data analysis, it is a clear indication that the hiring process needs improvement, and you need to onboard better-suited individuals who can confidently handle the job.

2 – RFP MANAGEMENT

To ensure that your clients do not miss out on critical details, it is crucial to invest in RFP management. Your sales operations team can be trained to place markers next to relevant and essential paragraphs, making it easier for your clients to focus on the most critical parts of the proposal. By implementing this practice, you can boost the chances of a successful close and feel confident that your clients receive the information they need to make an informed decision.

3 – WORK ON PROFESSIONAL DEVELOPMENT

By now, you must have realized that the success of your sales team hugely depends on the efficiency of your sales operation. However, your sales operation team might have employees with varying performance levels - some may be below average, some average, and some outstanding. To ensure your sales team's consistent growth and success, you must focus on the professional development of your sales team members, especially those who are average or below average. By providing them with professional development workshops, you can educate them about the industry you operate in, emerging trends, and the relevant technology that can help them maximize their success. This will enhance their skills and knowledge and boost their confidence, leading to greater productivity and better results.

4 – IMPLEMENT INTEGRATED BUSINESS SYSTEMS

One of the most well-recognized best practices in sales operations is to ensure that your team is proficient in using Sales Stack[4]. By implementing consistent dashboards across multiple software, you can empower your sales operations team to work cross-functionally and significantly improve data accuracy. With this approach, you can be assured that your sales operations will be streamlined and efficient, leading to better business outcomes and increased revenue.

If you are looking for top-notch tools to get your job done, then you should definitely consider Salesforce[5], Aviso[6], and Hoovers[7].

---

4 https://www.revenue.io/inside-sales-glossary/what-is-a-sales-stack
5 https://www.salesforce.com/
6 https://www.aviso.com/
7 https://www.dnb.com/products/marketing-sales/dnb-hoovers.html

Experts highly recommend these tools and are known for their exceptional performance.

KEY TAKEAWAY

Sales operation is a department with immense potential for growth and success. By implementing these four best sales operations practices, you can significantly boost your sales team's performance and achieve higher success rates. With these practices in place, you can be confident in the success of your sales operations.

CHAPTER 8

CONNECTING WITH CLIENTS

B oosting sales is not just about enhancing your products and services. While it is crucial to highlight the benefits and features of what you offer, building solid relationships with customers and clients is equally important. Connecting with them on a personal level can have a significant impact on your organization's growth, revenue, and profitability. So, do not just focus on the product; focus on the people who use it and watch your sales soar!

WHY IS IT IMPORTANT TO CONNECT WITH EXISTING CUSTOMERS?

Organizations cannot achieve any level of success, big or small, without their existing customers. Unfortunately, many employees in the sales department fail to recognize the true value of these customers, which is essential for their success. Organizations must prioritize and invest in their existing customer base to ensure sustainable growth and continued success.

To ensure customer loyalty, it is crucial to connect with existing customers. By establishing a strong relationship with them, you can guarantee their return to your business for all their needs and wants. Neglecting to prioritize your current customers can lead them to switch to a competitor, which is expensive and challenging to replace. Fortunately, catering to your existing customers is relatively simple since they already trust and are loyal to you. So, focus on nurturing your existing customer base to secure their unwavering loyalty.

HOW TO CONNECT WITH CLIENTS AND CUSTOMERS?

If you want to succeed in sales, knowing how to connect with your existing clients and customers is crucial. Thankfully, there are practical ways to do this. With the following three tips, you can engage with your customers, establish connections, and build strong relationships. These tactics will be valuable assets as you embark on your sales career.

1 – USE SOCIAL MEDIA

Social media has become a powerful tool for large FMCG companies to connect with their millions of users scattered all over the world. It enables them to engage with their audience on a global scale, creating a strong and lasting connection with every one of them.

Utilizing social media platforms such as X (Twitter), Instagram, TikTok, and Facebook is crucial to building and maintaining solid customer relationships. These platforms offer valuable insights into the content that your customers engage with, allowing you to tailor your approach to their interests and motivations. By leveraging these insights, you can understand your customers on a deeper level and foster a more meaningful connection with them.

Lastly, social media offers a powerful platform for sharing reviews. You can reach out to your clients and customers and request their valuable feedback to showcase on your business page. This can help you gain a deeper understanding of your customer's experience.

In case of any negative feedback, you can handle it confidently and take swift action to address the issue.

2 – SHARE STORIES

Sharing your story with your customers and clients can be as important as listening to their complaints, concerns, pain points, and requests. Do not be afraid to let them know who you are and what you stand for; it can help build trust and strengthen your relationship with them.

Sharing emotional stories about your products and services adds a human touch to your business and makes it more relatable. Many FMCG giants like Coca-Cola[8] have already adopted this strategy to connect better with their customers. By sharing relevant stories, your customers can relate to you and find common ground, which ultimately builds trust and fosters a stronger connection with your brand. So, do not hesitate to share your stories and create a more connected image for your business.

3 – KEEP YOUR CUSTOMERS INVOLVED

It is a fact that in today's world, people are more influential than brands. To establish a strong connection with customers, FMCG brands must harness the power of individuals to build their brand and develop a genuine connection with their consumers.

Nivea Men, a personal grooming company, launched a successful campaign in Malaysia to connect with its target audience. The campaign, named MYPadang, capitalized on the widespread popularity of football in the region by organizing a neighborhood football competition where local teams could compete against each

---

8 https://www.inmotionnow.com/project-workflow/storytelling-coca-cola-marketing/

other. As a result, Nivea Men saw a remarkable 20% increase in sales compared to the previous year.

Engaging and involving your brand with customers is crucial to establish a strong connection with them. Nivea Men's campaign perfectly demonstrates the significance of this approach.

KEY TAKEAWAY

Remembering that mutual respect, trust, and communication are the foundation of building robust and long-lasting customer relationships is essential. By effectively strengthening these pillars, you can be assured that your customers will remain loyal to your brand and continue choosing you over the competition.

CHAPTER 9

QUALIFYING PROSPECTIVE CLIENTS

It is of utmost importance for any sales employee to know how to qualify prospective clients effectively. As emphasized in Chapter 3, failing to identify the right prospective customers and clients can result in leaks from the Sales Funnel, ultimately wasting your time, efforts, and budget. With proper qualification techniques, you can ensure that you are focusing your energy on the most promising leads, leading to greater success and increased revenue.

Mastering the task of identifying and qualifying prospective clients is crucial for the success of your sales team. If you are facing challenges in doing so, do not worry! Here is a step-by-step guide that will help you tackle this task like a pro.

STEP 1 – PRECISELY DEFINE YOUR TARGET MARKET

To successfully qualify prospects, it is crucial to clearly understand your target market and communicate this effectively to your sales team. By identifying your ideal customer and focusing your efforts on prospects that align with your target, you will be able to hone in on the most promising opportunities for your business.

Here is a list of factors that you need to consider in this stage –

- Demographic
- Geography
- Company size

- Industry
- Budget
- Pain points

Having multiple buyer personas is absolutely acceptable and can be highly effective if done correctly. It is crucial to create detailed buyer personas that enable your sales team to focus on the most suitable prospects and weed out those who do not match your criteria. By doing so, you can boost your chances of success and achieve your sales goals.

By utilizing tools such as Google Analytics[9], you gain access to an 'Audience Tab,' which provides you with a wealth of information about your customers. With this knowledge, you can understand your customers, where they come from, and other vital details that can help you improve your business.

Note – When it comes to qualifying prospects, remember that not every lead will perfectly match your ideal customer profile. However, they must meet your basic, pre-defined criteria. With confidence in your process, you can effectively identify high-quality leads and focus your efforts on cultivating valuable relationships with them.

STEP 2 – FIND OUT WHAT THEY WANT

After identifying your target market, it is imperative to determine the product or service that will provide them with the greatest benefits.

To efficiently qualify prospects, your sales team must ask and uncover the answers to these four crucial questions:

---

9 https://analytics.google.com/analytics/web/

1. Do you require this particular product or service?

2. Will you be able to utilize our product or service effectively?

3. Are there any budget constraints? If yes, what is the maximum amount you can allocate?

4. Are you keen on purchasing our product or service?

Here are some additional questions to get a better understanding of the customer's decision-making process you may find helpful:

1. How do you plan to determine if our product or service is the right fit for your needs?

2. What factors do you consider when making a final decision?

3. Who else is involved in the decision-making process?

4. What would be your next step if you are satisfied with our offering?

STEP 3 – IDENTIFY AND ELIMINATE UNQUALIFIED LEADS QUICKLY

Now that you have gathered all the information from the previous step, you clearly understand which prospects fit your business best. Your next step should be to identify the clients who do not fit your target and eliminate them. This approach will save you valuable time and resources that can be better utilized for pursuing the right prospects. Remember, being confident in your decision-making will take you a step closer to achieving your business goals.

KEY TAKEAWAY

Investing time in educating your staff about your target market and the qualities that define an ideal customer is crucial. In addition, it is equally important to train your sales team to ask the appropriate questions during the qualification process, ensuring that prospects that do not meet the criteria are eliminated promptly, saving time and resources. This approach will help your business engage with the right prospects, increase conversion rates, and achieve sales targets.

CHAPTER 10

THE ART OF CREATING A WINNING SALES PITCH

O nce you have successfully identified and qualified the right leads, it is time for you to take charge and craft an unbeatable sales pitch. Your sales pitch can either make or break the deal, which makes it one of the most crucial aspects of your sales strategy. Therefore, you must approach it with confidence and the knowledge that it has the power to propel your business to new heights of success.

One of the biggest misconceptions about sales reps is that they are born with the gift of selling. However, this is not always the case. That is why it is essential to devote your time to preparing and refining your sales pitch before you meet your potential customer. Remember, your sales pitch will be your prospect's first impression of your business. So, you must put in a lot of effort to make it exceptional and leave a lasting impact.

Follow these guidelines to create a sales pitch that truly wins over your audience.

1 – DO YOUR RESEARCH

To deliver a compelling sales pitch, you must first conduct thorough research to understand your potential customers and their needs. By investing significant time and effort in researching your target audience, you will be better equipped to develop a sales pitch that speaks directly to their needs. This buyer-centric approach will significantly increase your chances of successfully closing a deal by effectively demonstrating how your product can add value to their lives. With the proper preparation and research, you can deliver a sales pitch that resonates with your audience and drives results.

To conduct effective research, it is crucial to thoroughly analyze the industry your client is operating in, study their company and competitors, and identify the primary decision-maker of the company. Armed with this knowledge, you can tailor your pitch to meet your customer's specific needs and successfully move the deal to the next phase.

2 – BUILD YOUR SALES PITCH AROUND A GOOD STORY

When it comes to crafting a successful sales pitch, one essential element is a compelling story. As human beings, we have an inherent affinity for narratives that resonate with us, and your potential customers are no exception. By utilizing storytelling in your sales pitch, you can effectively highlight the shared experiences and commonalities between you and your audience, helping to build a strong connection and increase the likelihood of a successful sale.

Great stories always have a personal touch that can evoke a powerful emotional response from the audience. Customers are drawn to stories that have a compelling narrative that showcases precisely how your product or service can benefit them. Therefore, crafting a sales pitch around a well-crafted story that clearly articulates the value of your product or service is crucial. With this approach, you can convey why your product or service is essential and how it can positively impact your customers' lives.

3 – PREPARE SHORT AND LONG VERSIONS OF YOUR PITCH

When it comes to sales, being prepared is vital. That is why it is important to have both a long and short version of your sales pitch ready to go. This way, you can easily adapt your message to any time constraints. If your prospective client tells you you only have 20 minutes to present, you can deliver your short pitch version. This should only take 5-15 minutes and include a maximum of 5 slides. And if necessary, you should also be ready to give the short version of the pitch without any slides at all. With this level of preparation, you can approach any sales situation with confidence and ease.

When it comes to pitching, the more extended version should be between 30 to 45 minutes long. If you have an hour-long meeting scheduled, do not hesitate to take up most of it with your sales pitch, leaving just a few minutes remaining for questions. Your pitch should consist of around 10 to 15 slides, and you should aim to spend no more than three minutes on each slide. With this approach, you can deliver a compelling presentation that will leave a lasting impact on your audience.

KEY TAKEAWAY

To make a great first impression on your client, it is crucial to deliver a confident and persuasive sales pitch. By following all the guidelines and preparing a stellar pitch, you can leave a lasting impression and increase your chances of closing the deal. So, go ahead and deliver your pitch with confidence and make it a memorable experience for your client.

CHAPTER 11

HANDLING REJECTIONS IN SALES

Sales rejections are a natural part of the sales process. Every successful salesperson has faced rejection at some point in their career. However, the ability to overcome rejections is what sets top-performing salespeople apart from the rest. With a winning mindset and the right strategies, salespeople can turn rejections into opportunities and achieve even greater success.

Rejections are an inevitable part of any sales career. But do not let them discourage you. Instead, embrace them as opportunities to learn and grow. You can turn any rejection into a stepping stone toward success with the right mindset and determination. As a sales professional, you have what it takes to overcome obstacles and achieve your goals.

Here are some tips that will help you handle rejections in your sales career best.

1 – EXPECT REJECTION AND DO NOT TAKE IT PERSONALLY

Just to reiterate, rejections are a natural part of sales. As a salesperson, you must train to remain confident and calm when a potential customer declines your offer. Remember, a "no" does not necessarily mean "never." Keep your head up and continue to pursue the next opportunity with unwavering confidence.

Moreover, rejection in sales does not necessarily mean that your product is not good enough or that you did not do your job well.

It simply means that the client had different requirements or expectations. It is also possible that they refused because of budget constraints. Always remember that rejection is not a personal attack, so do not let it get to you. Keep a positive attitude and use every opportunity to improve your sales technique.

2 – PLAN AND DELIVER GOOD RESPONSES

Rejections are an inevitable part of any career, and being prepared to handle them professionally is critical to becoming a top sales employee. With the right mindset, you can face any "no" that comes your way, armed with practiced responses that demonstrate your resilience and determination to succeed.

If a potential consumer mentions using a competitor's product, highlight how your existing consumer base has also initially used the same competitor's product. Emphasize how they eventually switched to your product when they discovered its increased benefits. You can even back up your claim with some powerful testimonials.

3 – REQUEST FOR FEEDBACK

To improve your product and increase customer satisfaction, it is crucial to seek feedback. By doing so, you can identify potential areas of improvement and rectify any issues that may have caused customers to reject your product. For example, consumers in the FMCG industry increasingly choose environmentally friendly products over non-sustainable ones. Therefore, it is essential to ask your customers why they did not select your product and take proactive measures to address their concerns.

4 – TALK TO YOUR TEAMMATES

If you are experiencing repeated rejections from customers, you should ask your more experienced team members for their advice. They can provide valuable strategies and tips to help you improve your sales pitch and boost your confidence. Practicing your pitch with them can also be a great way to prepare for future customer interactions.

5 – SOLVE THE PROBLEM

Based on the feedback you received earlier, you can proactively address the issue that led to rejections. For example, If plastic packaging is causing the problem, you could meet with your organization's Research and Development team to brainstorm eco-friendly packaging solutions. By taking this approach, you can demonstrate your commitment to sustainability while enhancing your product's appeal to potential customers.

However, if you are not receiving any feedback from your consumers, studying the leading brand or product in your category and gaining insights into what they are doing to drive better sales may be worthwhile. Doing this will allow you to enhance your product and minimize the risk of rejection.

KEY TAKEAWAY

Facing rejection is an inevitable aspect of sales, but as an aspiring sales professional, you must be confident in your abilities to handle it. With the proper set of skills in persuasion, negotiation, and unwavering persistence, you can overcome any rejection that comes your way and make progress in your sales career. Remember, confidence is vital to succeed in the world of sales.

CHAPTER 12

THE PERFECT WAY TO CLOSE A SALES DEAL

Closing a sales deal may seem straightforward in theory. You research, meet the customer, give your pitch, handle any queries, and close the sale. However, in practice, sales is more complex and requires a great deal of skill. It is not easy to avoid errors that could jeopardize a sales deal, particularly for beginners in this field. But with the right mindset and approach, you can confidently close a sales deal and succeed in your career.

If you want to be a master in sales, you need to master the art of closing a deal. It requires a perfect blend of science and art to close a sales deal successfully. Here are some techniques to help you develop the confidence and skills needed to close a deal like a pro.

1 – BE REAL

Establishing a sense of honesty and sincerity when dealing with potential customers is crucial. You can easily win their trust by demonstrating a genuine concern for their needs. During the sales process, it is essential to emphasize the benefits of your product or service. For example, if your business sells cooking oil and you are pitching to someone who is health-conscious, focus on the health benefits of your oil. By highlighting the positive aspects of your product, you can increase your chances of closing the deal.

To maximize your sales potential, it is essential to tap into the knowledge of your most loyal customers. By asking them why they choose to buy from you, you can identify key strengths and unique selling points to help you close deals effectively.

2 – CREATE A FEELING OF URGENCY

Establishing a sense of urgency in potential customers during a sales pitch is essential. One effective way to achieve this is by offering limited-time discounts or buy-one-get-one-free offers. As a sales representative or manager, you can leverage these offers to instill confidence in the customer that your product is the best choice for them and that they should act fast to take advantage of the opportunity. So, discuss a timeframe to encourage the customer to make an informed decision and choose your product over the competition.

3 – RESEARCH YOUR COMPETITORS

In the fast-moving consumer goods (FMCG) industry, competition is rife, and each player offers similar benefits or features. To stand out from the crowd and win over customers, you must identify the unique features of your product and use this knowledge to make a compelling case. This requires thorough research and preparation, enabling you to present your product with the utmost confidence and secure a successful close.

4 – ANSWER QUERIES

Being fully prepared to address and answer any potential queries can significantly boost your chances of closing a sales deal with confidence. It is highly recommended to have a well-organized outline of the most common questions and objections you may encounter and to have well-crafted answers prepared in advance.

By doing so, you can approach each sales situation assertively and with a greater likelihood of success.

KEY TAKEAWAY

Closing a sales deal is a breeze with the proper technique and preparation. Once you have mastered this art, achieving your KPIs and moving up the ladder to a promotion becomes a natural progression. You have got this!

CHAPTER 13

BUILDING LIFE-LONG RELATIONS WITH CUSTOMERS

Building a successful career in FMCG requires a deep understanding of the challenges associated with acquiring new customers. Despite the stiff competition, businesses and sales personnel put in a lot of effort to market their products and attract new customers. However, it is not enough just to make a sale, as customer loyalty is hard to come by in this industry. But with the right strategies and a strong brand image, businesses can retain customers and stay ahead of the competition.

Building strong customer relationships is essential for creating brand loyalty. When sales employees invest time and resources in nurturing these relationships, they can cultivate a dedicated customer base that remains loyal to the brand.

Here are some customer-building strategies that every sales employee needs to know.

STRATEGY 1 – FOCUS ON CUSTOMER RETENTION

Retention should be the number one priority for every sales employee in establishing enduring customer relationships. It is simpler to retain an existing customer and more cost-effective than acquiring new ones. Furthermore, by effectively managing your existing customer base, you can encourage them to return more frequently and make larger purchases from you. With a solid retention strategy in place, you can build a loyal customer base, boost revenue, and achieve long-term success.

To excel in sales, it is essential to prioritize repeat customers and focus your efforts on them. By implementing this strategy, you can expect to achieve higher revenues and profits and establish a loyal customer base that will drive your business forward.

STRATEGY 2 – EXCEED CUSTOMER'S EXPECTATIONS

Customers expect great products and services from the companies they choose to buy from. This rings especially true for FMCG companies that provide a myriad of everyday-use products. Therefore, your goal should be to work tirelessly to ensure the products you offer not only meet but surpass customer expectations.

In essence, let the quality of your product do the talking for you. Avoid making exaggerated claims during sales promotions. When customers experience exceptional quality products from you, their loyalty to your brand is assured, and they will keep coming back for more.

STRATEGY 3 – UNDERSTAND CUSTOMER PSYCHOLOGY

Only when you are able to understand your customer's needs comprehensively will you be able to deliver the products they need and increase customer satisfaction. You can analyze and understand customer psychology[10] based on their emotions and behaviors, which can help you serve them better.

---

10 https://www.quicksprout.com/consumer-psychology/

Understanding customer psychology is essential for building brand advocacy. By thoroughly understanding your customer's interests, preferences, likes, and dislikes, you can personalize your communications to resonate with them. For example, if a customer purchases your brand's shampoo, you can offer them ideas on how to style their hair after using it. This helps the customer to relate to your brand or product, which is crucial in building a loyal customer base. With such insights, you can confidently tailor your marketing strategies to meet their needs and create a lasting relationship with your customers.

STRATEGY 4 – CONNECT WITH CUSTOMERS

There are many ways to converse and speak with your customers. Using technology to communicate with your customers is an excellent way to connect with them and build strong relationships. Social media platforms are a powerful tool to help you reach out to your existing and potential customers. However, it is essential to remember that engaging with your customers should never be one-sided. You can keep your customers interested by asking relevant questions, encouraging them to comment and like your posts, and responding to their queries promptly. With these tips in mind, you can confidently connect with your customers and build lasting relationships.

KEY TAKEAWAY

As a sales employee in a highly competitive FMCG industry, it is crucial to develop long-lasting customer relationships. Building strong bonds with your customers makes them more likely to trust you and your brand, increasing sales and customer loyalty. So, prioritize customer relationship-building strategies to ensure your customers feel valued and confident in choosing your product over others.

CHAPTER 14

THE KEY TO BECOMING A SUCCESSFUL SALES COACH

Boosting sales performance through effective sales coaching is critical to successful sales management in every industry, including FMCG. However, many sales managers lack the necessary skills and expertise to provide their sales staff with the guidance and support they need to achieve their full potential.

Sales coaching is an essential component in building a successful sales team. It enhances their performance and equips them with the necessary tools to achieve their objectives. Experts view sales coaching as a behavior that encourages team members to assess themselves and discover effective problem-solving techniques, leading to significant growth opportunities.

To become a top-notch sales coach, you need to possess exceptional skills as a sales manager. With these skills, you can elevate your sales team's performance to new heights and significantly impact your organization's overall sales success. Here are proven ways to coach your sales team and help them achieve unparalleled success.

1 – ASK EFFECTIVE QUESTIONS

It is a well-established truth that people dislike being told what to do, even sales representatives. Therefore, a skilled sales coach should focus on establishing a consensus on the "what," which includes targets, goals, and objectives. They use strategic questioning to determine the "how," which involves the methods and techniques used to accomplish these objectives and achieve sales targets.

A successful sales organization empowers its sales force to take ownership of the solution, leading to improved execution and people development. Therefore, a high-performing sales coach should ask stimulating questions that inspire other sales team members to develop creative strategies and solutions.

2 – PROVIDE FEEDBACK ON PERFORMANCE

A competent sales coach takes a proactive approach towards delivering feedback to their team members based on their performance, ensuring they are always aware of their standing. It is important to note that feedback is not just about pointing out flaws and providing negative criticism.

The most effective sales coaches are confident in their abilities to give positive feedback. They proactively ensure their team members are aware of their strengths and achievements. Additionally, they recognize and commend the efforts of their best-performing salespeople and inspire others to strive for excellence.

3 – INCULCATE A SENSE OF PURPOSE

Sales coaches who are genuinely great share their vision with their sales team, providing a clear sense of direction that motivates them to work hard. They possess strong decision-making skills and are adept at bringing out the best in people through encouragement and support.

The top-performing coaches always look for ways to enhance the performance of their sales team. Their ability to combine complex data and emotional appeals is what drives people to take action.

4 – KEEP THE SALES FORCE FOCUSED

A successful sales coach exudes confidence and charisma, inspiring their sales team to stay laser-focused on achieving set goals and targets. They take the time to develop a clear and well-crafted action plan and go the extra mile to effectively communicate and ensure that their team fully understands and buys into it. With their unwavering confidence and effective communication skills, they lead their team to unparalleled success.

If you aspire to be a winning sales coach, you must be comfortable delegating duties and responsibilities to the right individuals. You must delegate tasks to knowledgeable and skilled individuals in that particular area rather than just anyone who happens to be available. Remember, your confidence in delegating will benefit you and help your team members grow and succeed.

5 – SPEND A LOT OF TIME IN THE FIELD

To become a great sales coach, being proactive and spending more time in the field is essential. Engaging in menial tasks such as clearing your email inbox is a waste of time and will not help you reach your full potential. So, focus your energy on the tasks that matter and take charge of your success.

To excel as a sales coach, it is imperative that you venture out of your office and actively coach your team. By closely observing your sales team's actions, you can identify their strengths and areas for improvement. Giving them constructive feedback can help them overcome obstacles and enhance their sales skills, leading them to greater success.

KEY TAKEAWAY

Becoming a successful sales coach is a nuanced process. Still, if you follow the strategies I have outlined above, you can be confident that you will see significant improvements in your sales team's performance. By asking effective questions, providing feedback, instilling purpose and focus, and holding your team accountable for successes and failures, you will be well on your way to achieving your goals. Remember, the best sales coaches are confident and resolute in their approach, knowing that their efforts will pay off in the end.

CHAPTER 15

EFFECTIVE SALES TRAINING TECHNIQUES

By following the guidelines in the previous chapter, you are well on your way to becoming a successful coach. Now, let us shift our focus to mastering the art of sales training. This chapter will provide the necessary tools and techniques to become a confident and effective sales trainer.

Many individuals use the terms "sales training" and "sales coaching" interchangeably. However, it is crucial to understand the fundamental differences between the two before delving into the intricacies of sales training techniques. By knowing how sales coaching and sales training differ, you can develop a sales strategy tailored to your specific business needs.

Mastering sales is a crucial aspect of any business, and sales coaching and sales training are two powerful tools that can help sales professionals achieve their goals. Sales coaching is tailored to address **individual-level** weaknesses and help sales professionals improve their skills. In contrast, sales training is designed to enhance the abilities of sales teams as a whole, at **group-level**, particularly new hires. Leveraging these two approaches allows sales professionals to build confidence and excel in their roles.

Sales training is a well-structured and efficient approach focusing on imparting specific concepts or skills to sales employees. It is one of the most effective ways to equip sales personnel with new skills, enabling them to overcome their weaknesses and perform better. Because of the structured nature of sales training programs, they are typically not conducted on a one-on-one basis.

Sales coaching is a crucial aspect of sales management, requiring managers to constantly monitor their team's performance and ensure they perform at their best. Unlike sales training, coaching is a personalized approach focusing on continuous growth and development of skills rather than just acquiring new knowledge. Sales coaching is often less formal and structured than sales training, emphasizing a more personalized approach to help sales teams achieve their full potential.

As a sales director or manager, it is your duty to equip your sales team with the tools they need to succeed. You must have a comprehensive and effective sales training program in place because what you teach your new hires will stay with them for a long time. It is crucial to ensure that you do this task correctly and efficiently. To help you with that, here are some guidelines for effective sales training.

1 – INVEST MORE TIME IN FIELD TRAINING

With field training, you can confidently unleash the full potential of your sales team. By providing them with a real-life experience, you're empowering them to achieve greater ROI[11] and drive success for your organization.

You must take your team to the field to provide them with the essential training and hands-on experience they need to succeed confidently. With continuous practice and guidance, your sales reps will master the selling process and learn to add innovation to their roles with ease.

---

11 https://www.allego.com/blog/capturing-the-roi-of-sales-training/

Pairing up an experienced sales representative with a junior one effectively guides them through the sales process. However, it is essential not to underestimate the capabilities of newly hired sales reps. They often bring fresh insights and creative ideas from the field that can enhance your training process.

2 – USE MOTIVATIONAL SUCCESS STORIES

Discussing theories and practices with sales reps to ensure a successful sales training program is insufficient. You must inspire them with real-life success stories, particularly from within your organization. By sharing these stories and identifying common themes and patterns in successful sales experiences, you can instill confidence and motivation in your new sales reps, setting them up for success.

Once you have shared a successful sales story with your team, it is crucial to emphasize the key takeaways that can be learned from it. Break down the process into practical steps that your team can easily implement in their sales pitches, and demonstrate how these techniques can be applied effectively in other aspects of the training process. By confidently highlighting these key takeaways, your team will be better prepared to replicate and build upon the success of the sales story.

3 – INCENTIVIZE WITH REWARDS

Like any other individual, intrinsic and extrinsic rewards can motivate sales professionals. Thus, it is crucial to establish clear and well-defined motivational rewards for them when they achieve specific milestones. Such rewards need not always be monetary bonuses or gift certificates; they could also include recognition for hard work or securing a top position in a friendly competition.

By setting up effective motivational rewards, you can create a more engaged and motivated sales team, leading to increased productivity and revenue.

As a sales manager, it is crucial to understand that motivating your team to perform better requires a deep understanding of their individual drivers. By gaining insights into what inspires them, you can confidently identify the rewards that will effectively incentivize their performance and drive success.

4 – USE THE MICRO-LEARNING APPROACH

Developing a competent sales force is a top priority for many managers. However, holding long meetings and bombarding sales reps with a large amount of information at once is ineffective. Sales reps cannot process and retain such an overwhelming amount of information. In fact, research shows that almost half of the information conveyed during sales training programs is lost within a few weeks unless it is consistently used on a daily basis. Therefore, it is vital to adopt a more strategic approach to sales training that promotes retention and utilization of information.

Contrarily, short meetings that allow employees to ask questions are an effective way to boost retention and interest. You can also adopt the TED Talks micro-learning model, where industry professionals and leaders share their insights and ideas in 15-minute sessions. This approach helps you train salespeople in manageable intervals, keeps them engaged, and helps them retain new information. I have used this method, which has made a significant difference in the effectiveness of the sales training program.

To ensure maximum productivity, it is essential to avoid over-training sales reps, as it can significantly impact their self-confidence. A micro-learning training approach employing small, frequent encouragement can help build confidence while preventing over-training.

KEY TAKEAWAY

Training your sales team can be a challenging task, but there are numerous effective ways to accomplish it. The key is to build a solid foundation for a culture of continuous learning and training. Fortunately, several sales training programs available today can help sales managers achieve this goal. Some of the most popular options include Sales Training and Strategy[12], The Art of Sales: Mastering the Selling Process Specialization[13], and IMPACT Sales Team Training[14]. With these resources at your disposal, you can feel confident that your sales team is receiving the best possible training to succeed in today's competitive market.

---

12 https://salesinsightslab.com/sales-strategy-consultant/
13 https://salesengine.com/who-we-are/
14 https://brooksgroup.com/sales-training/impact-sales-team-training-program

CHAPTER 16

MEASURING SALES PERFORMANCE

When sales targets are met successfully, it benefits everyone in the company. It improves the organization's profitability and positively impacts the sales reps' commissions and employee bonuses.

Measuring and monitoring your sales team's performance is crucial to managing your team and ensuring they meet their targets effectively. As a sales manager, it is essential to have clear and straightforward visibility into the performance of your entire team. This may seem daunting, but it is entirely achievable with the right tools and approach.

Becoming an effective sales manager requires taking actionable steps to build an efficient system for measuring, tracking, and reporting your sales team's performance. By implementing the following steps, you can develop a reliable system that ensures your sales team remains focused on achieving their goals. Get ready to lead your team with confidence.

STEP 1 – SET CLEARLY DEFINED GOALS AND EXPECTATIONS

Establishing well-defined goals and expectations for your team is the foundation for measuring sales performance effectively. With clear objectives in place, you can confidently track progress and make data-driven decisions to achieve greater success.

When setting targets, involving your entire sales team in the process is crucial. By doing so, you will better understand the obstacles they face and be able to set more practical and realistic goals. With this knowledge, your team will feel more motivated and driven to achieve their targets, resulting in increased productivity and overall success.

Thankfully, the market is brimming with online tools like ClickUp[15] and Milestone Planner[16] , designed to help you confidently define, set, and track your short-term and long-term business goals.

STEP 2 – PLAN TO MEASURE SHORT-TERM AND LONG-TERM GOALS

To achieve optimal results, it is crucial to maintain a dual focus on short-term and long-term goals when measuring performance. This approach has proven highly effective in promoting a positive work culture and driving success.

Consistently setting and achieving short-term goals is a great way to keep your team's progress on track. However, these goals can be subject to fluctuations that may demotivate your team. Amidst challenging times, it is important to have long-term goals that provide a more practical and realistic measure of success, giving your team the confidence to stay focused and achieve great things.

Likewise, it is not uncommon to encounter situations where short-term objectives are easily attained but long-term goals are stagnant. In such cases, it is crucial to evaluate micro-goals' efficacy in enabling sales representatives to accomplish their significant objectives.

---

15 https://clickup.com/
16 https://milestoneplanner.com/

STEP 3 – STAY UPDATED AT EVERY STAGE OF THE SALES FUNNEL

Your sales team must not only focus on closing sales deals successfully. They should also focus on every stage of the sales funnel, which involves tracking potential customers, qualifying leads effectively, and establishing long-lasting customer relationships. By doing so, they can ensure a more confident and sustainable growth for the business.

As a sales manager, it Is crucial to remember that you are not simply responsible for overseeing your team's sales pipeline. Instead, you are vital in guiding your team to lead customers through the pipeline effectively and efficiently. Trust your expertise and advise your team on best practices to ensure success.

Real-time metrics are essential to keep track of each sales representative's performance. This can be achieved by utilizing customizable dashboards, such as those offered by PowerBI[17]. These dashboards provide a comprehensive insight into your sales team's performance at every stage of the sales funnel, empowering you to make informed business decisions.

STEP 4 – FOLLOW UP WITH YOUR TEAM

To derive value from data, it is crucial to use it effectively for decision-making. You can drive positive outcomes and achieve success by generating insights and sharing them with your team.

One of the most effective ways to ensure that you and your team are always on top of things is to hold regular meetings. These meetings will allow you to discuss any upcoming or recurring problems, share troubleshooting solutions with the team, and even

---

17 https://powerbi.microsoft.com/en-us/

allow each member to share their unique creativity. By holding these meetings regularly, you can be confident that your team is always prepared to handle any challenges that come their way.

KEY TAKEAWAY

You can guide your team toward achieving their sales targets by utilizing the appropriate tools for measuring, tracking, and reporting performance.

CHAPTER 17

MOST IMPORTANT SALES KPIS

Sales Key Performance Indicators (KPIs) are powerful tools for evaluating sales teams' performance. They allow top sales management to quickly and accurately gauge the effectiveness and efficiency of sales activities within an organization. With these indicators, sales leaders can make confident and informed decisions that drive revenue growth and overall success.

Sales KPIs are essential for optimizing the sales funnel and performance. However, ensuring that the KPIs you track are relevant to your organization's business goals and the FMCG industry is crucial. Focusing on the right KPIs can help you maximize your resources while focusing on the wrong ones can lead to wasted resources. So, ensuring your organization tracks the right KPIs to achieve the desired results is crucial.

Below is a comprehensive list of the FMCG industry's most frequently used KPIs.

1 – MONTHLY SALES GROWTH

$$Monthly\ Sales\ Growth = \frac{Current\ Month\ Sales - Previous\ Month\ Sales}{Previous\ Month\ Sales} \times 100$$

I can confidently say that measuring the increase or decrease in sales revenue on a month-by-month basis is one of the most commonly used sales KPIs across almost every industry. It is a powerful tool for assessing any business's performance and identifying improvement areas.

By monitoring monthly sales growth, you can proactively review and take action on sales revenue trends in real-time instead of just reacting and analyzing past data. Setting achievable monthly sales revenue targets for your team and individual members will motivate them to perform better and ensure a cohesive and aligned sales effort across the organization.

2 – OUT OF STOCK RATE

$$Out\ of\ Stock\ Rate = \frac{Number\ of\ Items\ Out\ of\ Stock}{Number\ of\ Items\ in\ Stock} \times 100$$

With this KPI, you can measure your ability to meet customer demand in the Fast-Moving Consumer Goods (FMCG) industry. By identifying the time of day and week when your inventory goes out of stock, you can anticipate demand and supply your products in advance to ensure you never run out of stock. This KPI can also help you identify seasonal demand fluctuations, allowing you to make informed business decisions that give you a competitive edge in the market.

In the FMCG industry, managing inventory is critical as any product availability shortage can lead to potential customers choosing competitor products. This can result in lost sales and revenue for your organization. Therefore, it is essential to have a robust inventory management system in place to ensure your products are always available to your customers.

3 – AVERAGE TIME TO SELL

$$Average\ Time\ to\ Sell = \frac{Cost\ of\ Average\ Inventory}{Cost\ of\ Goods\ Sold} \times 365$$

In the FMCG industry, the speed at which products are sold is crucial due to their limited shelf life and expiration dates. This makes tracking the metric that indicates how quickly your products sell extremely important. Awareness of this metric will help you manage your inventory to ensure your products are always fresh and in high demand.

Understanding the exact time it takes to sell your product is crucial to strengthening your procurement strategies and improving inventory management. With this knowledge, you can confidently optimize your operations, reduce costs, and increase efficiency in areas such as storage, labor, and freight management.

4 – NUMERIC DISTRIBUTION PERCENTAGE

$$Numeric\ Distribution\ Percentage = \frac{Number\ of\ Stores\ Distributing\ Your\ Product}{Number\ of\ Stores\ Distributing\ this\ Product\ Category} \times 100$$

When it comes to sales measurement, the numeric distribution percentage is an absolutely crucial metric. It directly reflects the percentage of stores that carry your product in a particular area. Generally speaking, the higher the numeric distribution percentage, the better. However, if you work for a brand that selectively distributes its products, do not worry if you have a lower numeric distribution percentage, as this does not necessarily mean lower sales.

Utilizing this metric to evaluate how your product is positioned relative to your competitors is highly recommended for a more comprehensive analysis.

5 - WEIGHTED DISTRIBUTION PERCENTAGE

$$Weighted\ Distribution\ Percentage = \frac{Turnover\ of\ Stores\ Distributing\ Your\ Product}{Number\ of\ Stores\ Distributing\ this\ Product\ Category} \times 100$$

When it comes to assessing the sales performance of a product category, comparing its sales turnover with that of stores selling a similar product from the same category is a key metric. This KPI can be measured globally or on an area-wide basis, providing valuable insights into the overall sales trend.

As a sales manager, it is crucial to prioritize placing your product in stores that consistently generate a higher percentage of sales turnover. Your objective should be to surpass the numeric distribution percentage by achieving a higher weighted distribution percentage, thereby ensuring optimal product placement and sales performance.

6 – SALES VOLUME BY LOCATION

$$Sales\ Volume\ by\ Location = \frac{Cost\ of\ Goods\ Sold\ in\ A\ Particular\ Location}{Total\ Cost\ of\ Goods\ Sold} \times 100$$

By analyzing the sales volume across various locations, such as brick-and-mortar stores and online platforms, you can confidently identify the areas where your product has high and low demand. This information will help you make informed decisions to optimize your sales strategy and increase revenue.

Based on this data, you can identify discrepancies across different locations and devise practical and effective solutions to increase demand in areas where your product may not perform well.

KEY TAKEAWAY

Measuring KPIs is crucial, but it is just the first step. After calculating the KPIs, you need to analyze them to understand your results comprehensively. Then, you can identify ways to improve your performance on these metrics and follow through with action. Remember that KPIs are only meaningful when linked to an overarching goal, so stay focused on your approach, tackle challenges head-on, and make the necessary adjustments to achieve your desired outcomes.

CHAPTER 18

BOOSTING SALES PRODUCTIVITY

Optimizing sales efforts' outcomes while minimizing expenses is essential to achieving sales productivity. In other words, your sales team can be considered truly productive when it is able to sell more, generate higher revenues, and efficiently utilize time and money.

Boosting sales productivity is a challenging task, but not impossible. According to a study by The Bridge Group[18] in 2017, one of the most prominent challenges sales managers face is enhancing sales performance and productivity. However, the right strategies and tools can overcome these challenges and achieve remarkable sales growth.

WHAT LEADS TO LOW SALES PRODUCTIVITY

Several factors can contribute to low sales productivity, but these challenges can be overcome with the right approach and mindset, such as:

- Inconsistent sales processes and strategies can be overcome by streamlining and optimizing processes.

- Excessive pressure to surpass sales targets can be overcome through effective time management and goal-setting techniques.

---

18 https://blog.bridgegroupinc.com/hubfs/resources/2017_SaaS_AE_Metrics.pdf?t=1525961943442

- Lack of communication from senior management can be overcome through proactive measures.

- Failure to prioritize sales activities can be overcome through careful planning and analysis.

- Inadequate investment in sales training and coaching practices can be overcome by organizations prioritizing training and coaching to equip their sales teams with the skills and knowledge needed to succeed in today's competitive marketplace.

- Negative sales culture with poor internal communication, increased competition, office gossip, and lack of discipline can be overcome by fostering a positive sales culture through open communication, teamwork, and a commitment to professional development.

- Frequent external distractions can be overcome through effective time management and focus.

- Poorly defined target markets can be overcome by carefully researching and defining target markets.

- Resistance to adopting innovative sales technologies and tools can be overcome by embracing innovative sales technologies and tools to stay ahead of the curve and build sustainable competitive advantages.

- Poor route planning and scheduling. Organizations must optimize route planning and scheduling to maximize efficiency and reduce wasted time and resources.

- Turnover and unpredictable demand patterns can be overcome with the right strategies and approach.

Undoubtedly, some factors can pose challenges to achieving sales productivity, but it is essential to remember that solutions are always available. Organizations can confidently overcome these challenges and achieve sustainable growth and success by implementing effective strategies and solutions to address obstacles like poor route planning and scheduling or negative sales culture. With the right approach and mindset, anything is possible.

No matter the size of the hurdle, one thing is certain - members of your sales team are equipped to overcome any challenge thrown their way. In today's competitive sales environment, there is little tolerance for mistakes, but with their expertise and confidence, your team will surely succeed.

STRATEGIES TO BOOST SALES PRODUCTIVITY

To boost your sales team's productivity, focus on these key pillars that can serve as the stepping stones toward success. Embrace a positive attitude and look at the brighter side of things to create a more confident and effective sales force.

1-CONSISTENCY

To maintain consistency in sales practices, procedures, and policies, it is imperative to have a well-defined organizational structure. The structure provides a clear framework that ensures the sales team operates with confidence and certainty, resulting in better performance and outcomes.

2-FOCUS

Eliminating practices that distract your sales team from their goals is a crucial aspect of sales management. According to a study by McKinsey Global Institute, the average person spends around 13 hours of their week only on email[19], which accounts for more than 25% of their entire work week. By addressing this issue head-on,

19 https://www.mckinsey.com/industries/high-tech/our-insights/the-social-economy

you can ensure your sales team stays focused and confident in achieving their targets.

To tackle these challenges, a highly effective approach is temporarily turning off email and chat platforms during specific periods of the day. Additionally, it is recommended to impose a limitation on sales reps, allowing them to respond to emails for only 30 minutes at a time, following which they can redirect their focus back to their core sales duties.

3-CONTINUOUS INNOVATION

I firmly believe it is crucial to ask yourself this question: "Are your sales tools and processes highly efficient and effective?"

Investing in innovative tools and technology is crucial as the sales industry evolves rapidly. Failing to do so can significantly hinder your sales team's productivity and may put your business at a disadvantage in the highly competitive market.

Sales representatives can boost their productivity by using route planning apps like Badger Mapping[20] to find the shortest route to their daily sales appointments. This helps them save time and focus on what truly matters - closing deals and generating revenue.

4-REDUCE PRESSURE

Sales managers often put undue pressure on their teams to achieve better sales targets. What they overlook is that even the best salespeople can face a slump in their performance from time to time. It is important to remember that the key to success lies in striking a balance between motivation and pressure.

---

20 https://www.badgermapping.com/

As a competent sales manager, it is crucial to understand that while motivating your sales team to perform at their best, exerting excessive pressure on them can hamper their productivity. Therefore, it is imperative to balance motivating and pressuring them to ensure optimal performance.

To ensure your top sales employees are performing at their best, it is crucial to communicate with them and understand the root cause of any underperformance. Additionally, it is important to regularly evaluate the sales targets given to your employees to ensure they are challenging yet achievable. When your sales team believes their quotas are realistic, they are more likely to put in the necessary effort to achieve them, resulting in greater success for your business.

KEY TAKEAWAY

To be a successful sales manager, you must confidently lead your team to maximize their productivity while ensuring their happiness and engagement. Remember that a happy and engaged sales team can increase productivity by 31% and generate 37% more sales. So, be confident in your approach and lead your team to success.

CHAPTER 19

SALES LEADERSHIP

It is common for individuals to mistake the concept of sales leadership for the sales management role. Still, it is essential to recognize that these two aspects have distinct differences.

Sales leadership is the art of spotting opportunities others cannot see and taking advantage of them to achieve remarkable results. Conventional norms do not bind a sales leader who is always looking to innovate and bring about change. No matter the situation, they possess an unrelenting drive to learn and grow.

Sales leadership is a fascinating topic, and it is crucial to differentiate it from sales management. Let us explore what sets these two apart and why sales leadership is critical for success in any sales organization.

SALES LEADERSHIP VS. SALES MANAGEMENT

Sales leaders inspire, while sales managers strive to improve. That is the fundamental difference between the two.

At its core, successful sales management requires a clear vision and direction and effective communication that is primarily one-way in nature. In contrast, effective sales leadership is built on the foundation of understanding the importance of two-way communication. A genuinely great sales leader always inspires their team to speak up frequently and share their opinions and concerns rather than just complying with orders in silence.

Sales managers prioritize closing sales and offer guidance to their sales team to achieve this goal. While concerned with the numbers, sales leaders prioritize their team members' emotional and mental well-being.

WHAT MAKES A GOOD SALES LEADER?

Effective sales leadership relies more on soft skills than hard skills. The key is possessing the right qualities and traits to inspire, motivate, and lead a team towards success. Here are some top qualities a sales leader should have to achieve that goal.

1 –PROVIDE FEEDBACK

A great sales leader's most effective habit is providing their team with immediate and effective feedback.

Sales leaders can use the three-part approach to give feedback effectively, following the BIG acronym. This method involves discussing a specific behavior, explaining its impact, and ensuring an agreement is reached to modify the behavior. This approach has proven to be one of the most effective ways of providing feedback in the sales industry.

2 – BUILD TEAM SPIRIT

Managing a sales team with low morale can be daunting, but it is not impossible. Low morale among sales employees can lead to poor performance and disengagement. However, with the right approach and effective leadership, it is possible to turn things around and create a motivated and high-performing team.

Influential sales leaders prioritize building team spirit as a critical factor for success. Rather than letting low morale hold their team back, they proactively identify disengaged sales reps and diagnose the root cause of their dissatisfaction. With a clear understanding of the problem, they develop and implement targeted strategies to re-energize and motivate their team, resulting in a more effective sales force.

3 – ADAPT COACHING STYLES

Successful sales leaders understand the importance of tailoring coaching styles to suit the unique needs of each salesperson. They recognize that there are a variety of selling styles that can lead to success and avoid using a one-size-fits-all approach. By adapting their coaching style to the individual, these leaders foster an environment of confidence and inspire their team to achieve greater success.

4 – LEVERAGE STRENGTHS

Based on extensive research conducted by Gallup, it has been proven that focusing on and investing in employees' strengths can significantly increase employee engagement - up to 8 times more.

As highly successful sales leaders, it is crucial to regularly evaluate the strengths of all team members using powerful tools like CliftonStrengths[21] and Standout[22]. This way, we can leverage the insights gained to drive exceptional results and achieve our goals.

Based on the Standout model's assessment of an employee as a Teacher, the sales leader can confidently suggest that they conduct internal product training to leverage their strengths fully.

---

21 https://www.gallup.com/cliftonstrengths/en/252137/home.aspx
22 https://www.tmbc.com/standout/

KEY TAKEAWAY

To meet sales goals, exceptional sales leaders understand that they need to focus on their team's development. They can ensure peak performance and drive better results by continuously honing their employees' skills. In doing so, leaders can foster loyalty among top performers and achieve long-lasting success.

CHAPTER 20

STAYING OPTIMISTIC

Sales employees who can maintain a positive and optimistic attitude even when facing challenges are more likely to succeed. In fact, according to many experienced sales managers, the ability to stay optimistic is the top trait that sets successful salespeople apart.

Staying optimistic and motivated is crucial for success. When sales are low, keeping your sales team motivated can be challenging. However, staying positive and leading by example can inspire your team to work hard and achieve great results. Remember that challenges are opportunities to grow and learn, and with the right mindset, anything is possible.

Fortunately, it is quite simple to adopt an optimistic mindset. Let me share some tips with you on how you can keep your team and yourself optimistic.

1 – WRITE DOWN YOUR GOALS

As a sales team member, having a clear vision of your trajectory is crucial. Ask yourself the following questions:

- What are your primary goals?
- Where do you see yourself in the long run?

By writing down your objectives, you will be empowered to push through challenges when uncertain about your path.

Always keep a notebook handy and make it a daily habit to write down your goals as part of your morning routine. Encourage your sales team to do the same, as it will help keep them aligned with their objectives and prevent any distractions from getting in the way of achieving success. By staying committed to your goals and prioritizing them daily, you can confidently move closer to achieving them.

2 – CREATE A VISION BOARD

Visualizing your goals through vision boards is an incredibly effective method to stay focused and motivated. Whether you prefer a physical or digital format, a well-crafted vision board can help you manifest your dreams and achieve your life's significant milestones. Fill it with images of your desired travel destinations and personal achievements, and watch yourself take charge of your future.

Keeping a vision board in sight will constantly remind you of your goals and aspirations, fueling your determination to achieve them.

3 – FOCUS ON SOLUTIONS

You can easily achieve a positive mindset by shifting your focus towards solutions instead of dwelling on the problems. The more you concentrate on finding solutions, the quicker you can tackle any obstacle.

Instead of worrying about not getting enough leads, why not take action and attend an upcoming networking event to generate leads? Adopting a proactive approach can cultivate a mindset to help you achieve your goals.

4 – EMBRACE THE NO'S

Receiving 'No's is a natural aspect of sales, and it is essential to embrace them.

One way to do this is to recognize that sales is a numbers game, meaning that every "No" you receive leads you closer to a "Yes." With this mindset, you can approach each rejection, knowing that it is all part of the process of achieving success.

5 – TURN ON YOUR FAVORITE PLAYLIST

When boosting your motivation and confidence, a killer play-list can work wonders. Whether you need to power through a demanding workday or get energized for an important meeting, nothing beats the uplifting power of music. So, if you want to conquer any challenge with a can-do attitude, turn up the volume on motivational tunes and let them fuel your success.

If you want to elevate your energy levels, I highly recommend checking out the following artists: Government Mule, Tool, and Aerosmith. They will surely get you pumped up and ready to take on the day!

6 – THINK OF YOUR MISTAKES AS LEARNING EXPERIENCES

Mistakes are valuable lessons that allow us to gain the experience and confidence needed to succeed.

Listing down your most common mistakes can be a great way to recognize and overcome them. Do not be afraid to speak with your manager or coworkers about improving. Alternatively, you can find helpful resources like YouTube videos to guide you. With the right mindset and resources, you can tackle any challenge.

KEY TAKEAWAY

If you want to achieve your goals in life, it is up to you to take responsibility. Do you not like your current situation? Take action and change it! The key to bringing about change is having a positive and optimistic mindset. Believe in yourself and your abilities, and you will be amazed at what you can accomplish.

CHAPTER 21

SERVICE – THE KEY TO EFFECTIVE SALES

C ustomer service is the cornerstone of any successful business, regardless of the industry. A top-notch customer service team enhances the customer experience and fosters a powerful and long-lasting relationship between a business and its customers.

I am confident that customer service plays a crucial role in the success of a sales department. Not only does it lead to happy customers, but it also helps build a better reputation, ultimately leading to increased growth. According to Research[23], 69% of customers who have a positive experience with a company are likely to recommend it to others.

In addition to being crucial for customer satisfaction, a top-notch customer service is a powerful tool for cultivating customer loyalty. When customers have a positive experience with your product or service, they are more likely to remain steadfast to your brand. It is well-established that retaining existing customers is far more cost-effective than acquiring new ones. As a result, the higher the lifetime value of a customer (i.e., the total revenue a business can expect from a single customer during their relationship with the business), the greater the profits for your business. By providing exceptional customer service, you can boost your brand's reputation and retain customers who will generate revenue for your business in the long run.

---

23 https://www.groovehq.com/customer-service-statistics

Research unequivocally demonstrates that superior customer service can significantly impact a business's financial bottom line. In fact, a staggering 86% of customers[24] are willing to pay up to 25% more for companies that deliver exceptional customer service. This statistic clearly indicates the immense value of customer service and how it can be a crucial differentiator for businesses that strive to provide top-notch service to their customers.

Customer service is crucial for any organization, and building a dream team that can deliver exceptional customer service is vital to success. Let us explore how your organization can create a customer service dream team to exceed your customers' expectations.

1 – ENCOURAGE YOUR SALES TEAM TO PRIORITIZE QUICK AND ACCURATE RESPONSES

According to research conducted by Oracle[25], over half of Facebook and 80% of Twitter users anticipate receiving a response to their inquiries within 24 hours or less. Some other surveys even indicate that customers demand a response within an hour.

A swift response is important, but it is only half the battle. The key to effective customer service is resolving the problem effectively and efficiently. It is vital to ensure that the customer's issue is fully resolved the first time around so they do not have to reach out again for the same problem.

2 – EMPOWER YOUR EMPLOYEES

Once you have hired the perfect candidate for your customer service team, trust in their abilities and provide them with the necessary

---

24 https://www.slideshare.net/RightNow/2011-customer-experience-impact-report
25 http://www.oracle.com/us/products/applications/commerce/live-help-on-de-mand/oracle-live-help-wp-aamf-1624138.pdf

tools and authority to make quick and sound decisions. This way, when customers have inquiries, they can receive prompt and assertive responses without experiencing prolonged wait times.

3 – LISTEN TO YOUR CUSTOMERS

As a sales employee, it is crucial to prioritize listening to your customers' grievances. It may seem obvious, but you would be surprised how many businesses fail to follow this basic rule. According to a 2015 report by Forrester on customer experience[26], only 1% of businesses were found to provide excellent customer service. By assuring your customers that they are in safe hands, you can differentiate yourself from the competition and build a loyal customer base.

4 – RESPECT THE CUSTOMER'S TIME

Efficient customer service is a top priority for businesses. Customers always have a specific issue they want to resolve, and as a business, you are responsible for providing them with the best support possible. When a customer contacts your support team, it is crucial to ensure that unnecessary hurdles do not waste their valuable time. By promptly addressing their queries and concerns, you can demonstrate your passion for providing top-notch customer service.

5 – ASK RELEVANT QUESTIONS

Gathering as much information as possible is essential to resolve a customer's issue successfully. Do not hesitate to ask questions and collect all the necessary details to propose alternate solutions.

---

26 https://www.forrester.com/report/The+US+Customer+Experience+Index-+Q1+2015/-/E-RES117482

Remember, the more information you have, the more effective you will be in resolving the customer's issue.

KEY TAKEAWAY

Providing excellent customer service has become more straightforward, thanks to digitization. However, as customers become more empowered, it is crucial to have an appropriate protocol in place to ensure consistent delivery of great experiences and service. With confidence in your approach, you can proactively address any concerns before they escalate and guarantee your customers are always satisfied.

CHAPTER 22

USING TECHNOLOGY TO BOOST SALES

With technological advancements, we have the power to revolutionize the sales process and take it to unprecedented heights. The benefits offered by technology are endless - from building stronger customer relationships to converting qualified prospects into loyal customers. It is the key to unlocking the true potential of sales. Not only does technology offer numerous benefits, but it also empowers you to upgrade the sales communication process and showcase your organization's products with utmost efficiency.

Here are some of the latest tools and technologies that can help you boost sales and make your organization stand out.

1 – CUSTOMER RELATIONSHIP MANAGEMENT TOOLS

Using CRM tools like the Hubspot CRM[27] is invaluable for skyrocketing your sales. These tools keep your business's systems and information in one central location, which can significantly improve company-wide communication, foster better alignment between Marketing and Sales teams, and ultimately boost engagement with prospective customers.

In addition, implementing CRM tools will enable your sales team to access various sales tools seamlessly. For instance, they can

---

27 https://www.hubspot.com/products/crm

leverage social media tools[28] to precisely target, market, and sell to potential customers on social media platforms.

With the help of a robust CRM system, your salesforce can optimize their daily schedules and prioritize tasks to ensure that customers are not neglected and significant prospects are contacted on time. By leveraging powerful CRM tools, your salesforce can spend more time with customers, leading to more closed deals and a more substantial customer base.

Capitalizing on the power of CRM tools is absolutely essential for ensuring high levels of customer satisfaction. With all the relevant customer data stored in CRM, your salesforce can quickly analyze customer demands and anticipate any issues they may face. This boosts customer satisfaction and strengthens customer loyalty, ultimately leading to increased profitability.

2 – VIDEO AND SCREEN-SHARING TOOLS

In a sales organization, video conferences are vital in accomplishing a lot of work. Therefore, video and screen-sharing tools are of utmost importance. With the likes of Skype, Zoom[29], Microsoft Teams, and Google Meet, sharing product demos, and educational and marketing content has become seamless and effortless.

3 – SALES REPORTING TOOLS

Sales reporting software, like Power BI for Office 365[30], empowers your sales team to track and analyze multiple sales metrics and data points accurately. Using these tools, your team can measure their individual and group success, quickly identify areas for im-

---

28 https://www.hubspot.com/products/marketing/social-inbox
29 https://zoom.us/
30 https://powerbi.microsoft.com/en-us/blog/tag/office-365/

provement, and gain valuable insights into which sales techniques are most effective and which need refinement.

4 – PRODUCTIVITY TOOLS

Selling virtually or remotely can be challenging, especially when your sales team has to juggle multiple tasks, such as responding to emails, managing to-do lists, and communicating with other team members. However, with the help of productivity tools like Taskful[31] and Things[32], your sales team can efficiently manage their time and focus on closing deals. This increases your sales team's productivity and boosts their confidence in handling multiple tasks simultaneously.

KEY TAKEAWAY

To find the sales tool that perfectly fits your team, thoroughly research the various sales tools and technologies available.

---

31 https://taskful.com/
32 https://culturedcode.com/things/

CHAPTER 23

SALES IN AN FMCG INDUSTRY

F MCG sales, or fast-moving consumer goods sales, is a fascinating field requiring strong relationship-building and management skills. It is an area where confidence is vital, and successful salespeople thrive on the challenge of building and maintaining long-lasting partnerships with their clients.

HOW DO FMCG SALES WORK

Without a doubt, the business-to-business (B2B) aspect of FMCG sales holds the utmost importance. Sales professionals working in this area take charge and actively schedule and participate in meetings with the purchasing department of retail outlets. They confidently demonstrate their product and skillfully persuade buyers to make bulk purchases.

On the other hand, the business-to-consumer (B2C) aspect of FMCG sales targets the end consumer. This can be achieved either by retail selling or via direct sales, such as door-to-door selling.

SUCCESSFUL FMCG SALES TECHNIQUES

Here's how you can achieve success in FMCG Sales.

1 – HAVE A CLEARLY LAID OUT SALES PLAN

You need a sound strategy and an excellent sales plan to succeed in FMCG sales. As you develop your sales plan, cover all aspects, including:

102

- Setting realistic deadlines and targets

- Building traction for your target market

- Defining your Unique Selling Point or competitive advantage

- Leveraging relationships with current clients

With a well-rounded plan, you can drive your FMCG sales towards success.

2 – OPTIMIZE YOUR SALES ROUTE

By utilizing a map, such as Google Maps, you can confidently develop an easy-to-follow sales route that will allow you to optimize your existing resources and expand your business. Optimizing your sales route can offer numerous benefits, including maximum coverage of stores and retailers with minimum vehicles, timely delivery, lower costs, and increased savings. Additionally, you can equip your salesforce with powerful tools, such as Route XL[33], Batch Geo[34], and Mapline[35], to optimize their supply routes and further increase their efficiency.

3 – UTILIZE MAXIMUM SHELF SPACE

Consistent analysis and monitoring of your product's performance and in-store shelf conditions for your brand and competitors are crucial for achieving success. Maximizing your shelf space utilization can be easily achieved through two simple steps:

- Gauge your shelf performance

- Use high-quality display tools

---

33 https://www.routexl.com/
34 https://batchgeo.com/
35 https://mapline.com/

- Identify areas of improvement in shelf utilization

Utilizing shelf space can take your brand's performance to new heights.

4 – MONITOR YOUR STOCK

In the FMCG industry, inventory is the most valuable asset. As a sales team member, ensuring that your department closely monitors the stock of all available products across each location is crucial. To accomplish this, you must:

- Have excellent control over inventory and use effective and practical tools such as Megaventory[36] or Zoho Inventory[37].

- Avoid overstocking your product.

- Guarantee that your stock is visible at all stores across every location.

- Invest in top-notch inventory management tools such as inFlow Inventory[38] and Odoo[39].

With these strategies and tools, you can be assured that your sales team will easily track inventory, allowing maximum efficiency and profitability.

5 – IMPLEMENT A SALES FORCE AUTOMATION SOFTWARE

Investing in a powerful sales force automation software that includes all the above points is a surefire way to boost your sales and revenue. With a top-of-the-line sales force automation tool

---

36 https://www.megaventory.com/
37 https://www.zoho.com/inventory/
38 https://www.inflowinventory.com/
39 https://www.odoo.com/app/inventory

such as Freshsales[40], Pipedrive[41], and Salesforce[42], you can expect to have access to an array of features, including:

- KPI tracking
- Geo-tagging features
- Built-in distributor management systems
- Scheme management and order management

By leveraging such tools, you can focus on generating more sales and increasing your revenue without worrying about the complexities of managing your sales force.

KEY TAKEAWAY

Your sales team must adopt these tactics as they have been proven to be highly effective in boosting sales!

40 https://www.freshworks.com/crm/sales/

41 https://www.pipedrive.com/

42 https://www.salesforce.com/

CHAPTER 24

B2C VS B2B SELLING

F MCG sales are primarily comprised of B2B and B2C sales. In the previous chapter, we briefly discussed these two types of sales. This chapter will delve deeper into B2B and B2C sales, as they are crucial components of the FMCG industry.

B2B SELLING

In B2B sales, you must deeply understand your product and its features to communicate its value to your potential buyers effectively. As you will be dealing with retail outlets, your primary focus will be on these businesses' Purchasing Department or Buying Manager.

One key aspect of B2B sales is that buying decisions are based purely on business needs, without personal emotion. Therefore, it is essential to understand your buyer's requirements, how they operate within their organization's practices, and their role in decision-making.

To succeed in B2B sales, your focus should be on how your product can benefit the potential buyer's business. You should be able to articulate the level of return on investment your buyer can expect from purchasing, stocking, and selling your product. With a deep understanding of your product and buyer's needs, you can position your product as the best solution to meet their business requirements.

B2C SELLING

Regarding B2C selling, the direct selling approach to the end consumer is critical. You can set up your retail outlet to showcase your products or sell door-to-door. In today's world, where FMCG products are primarily sold online, creating your online store and selling directly to the end consumer is essential.

Focusing on your product's benefits is crucial when selling products to consumers. The decision-making process, in this case, is more emotional than rational. Additionally, selling to consumers requires multiple distribution channels to make buying more convenient. Consumers are not interested in long marketing messages and expect you to get to the point quickly. They want you to point out the benefits of your product rather than figuring it out on their own.

In B2C sales, your message must be crisp, easy, and simple to understand. Your sales strategies should be solely focused on the benefits your product provides. Therefore, it is essential to highlight the main problem or pain point that your product aims to solve. With the right approach, you can confidently sell your products to the end consumer and establish a strong presence in the market.

KEY TAKEAWAY

It is a common misconception that B2C sales take precedence over B2B sales in the FMCG industry because of the nature of fast-moving consumer goods. However, this could not be further from the truth. In reality, B2B sales are much more vital than B2C sales, even in the FMCG industry. This is due to the fact that your product will be sold and stocked at thousands of retail outlets, which are essentially businesses. As a result, to reach the consumer, it is imperative to collaborate with businesses and ensure that your B2B strategies are effective and successful.

CHAPTER 25

THE JOB DESCRIPTION OF AN FMCG SALES MANAGER

This chapter will explore a sales manager's essential roles and responsibilities in an FMCG company. As a Sales Manager in an FMCG company, you will be the driving force behind the sales of your company's products. Your primary responsibility will be to increase sales by expanding the existing customer base and bringing in new customers. You will excel in a specific area of consumer goods, such as personal care or home goods, and cater to a range of customers, such as large retailers, wholesalers, businesses, shops, or individuals across your specified geographical area.

As a Sales Manager, you will lead a sales team by providing them with the necessary training, guidance, and mentorship to succeed. Setting sales targets, goals, and quotas, developing sales plans, assigning sales territories, analyzing data, and building a team will all be a part of your job responsibilities. These tasks require a high level of confidence, and you must be able to make informed decisions and take calculated risks to achieve your goals.

This is how an FMCG company usually advertises a vacancy for a Sales Manager:

"Our fast-growing FMCG company is hiring! As our Sales Manager, you will be the driving force behind our sales success. You will be responsible for creating effective business plans, achieving ambitious targets, and working closely with our Marketing Department to generate leads. You will also be in charge of monitoring the performance of your sales team, setting goals, and providing training to ensure they are at the top of their game. Join us and take your sales career to new heights."

ROLES AND RESPONSIBILITIES OF A SALES MANAGER

As a Sales Manager, your job description would typically include the following tasks:

- Developing and executing effective sales strategies to meet the overall business goals.

- Leading and managing the sales team to achieve sales growth and meet sales targets.

- Collaborating with team members and other departments, including Finance and Marketing, to implement strategic sales plans.

- Fostering customer engagement practices.

- Monitoring and tracking the performance of individuals.

TOP SKILLS AND QUALIFICATIONS

To thrive as a Sales Manager, you must be equipped with the qualifications, experience, and skills to fulfill the key responsibilities.

- A Bachelor's degree in Business or any related field, such as Marketing, Finance, Accounting, or Administration, is typically required.

- Mid or senior-level experience.

- You should possess excellent communication and leadership skills to spearhead objectives and strategies for the entire department.

- Attending meetings and developing innovative sales practices should be second nature to you.

- You should have a strong ability to understand financial trends and work with numbers and graphs, allowing you to make accurate reports and forecasts easily.

CAREER PATH

If you aspire to become a Sales Manager, securing a Bachelor's degree in Business Administration, Marketing, or any other related field is the first step toward achieving your goal. While pursuing your degree, participate in part-time jobs or internships in the sales department of an FMCG company to gain hands-on experience. Once you have completed your degree and have some experience working in sales, you can apply for the role of an Assistant Sales Manager at FMCG companies. With some more experience in this role, you will be fully equipped to take on the position of a Sales Manager and excel in your career.

With around 7-8 years of experience as a Sales Manager, you can expect to be promoted to a higher sales leadership position. Your next role is typically that of a Sales Director, followed by Vice President of Sales, Chief Revenue Officer, and ultimately Chief Operating Officer or Chief Executive Officer.

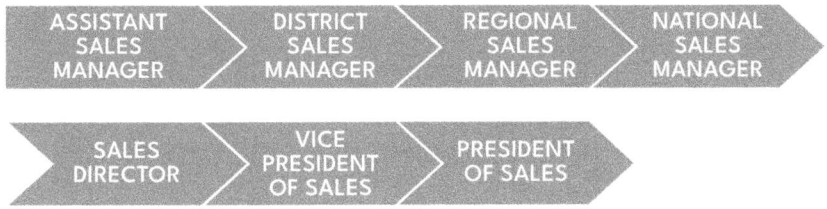

SALARY GUIDE

Based on reliable data from Indeed[43], the average base salary for Sales Managers in the US stands at an impressive $80,061 per year. As if that is not enough, Sales Managers are also entitled to receive bonuses of up to $15,000 cash bonus per year, plus a whopping $24,000 commission annually.

When it comes to top FMCG companies like Procter and Gamble, Sales Managers can expect to earn an enviable base pay ranging from $77,000 to $149,000 per year. This means the total pay package can go as high as $149,000 annually, depending on the experience level and expertise.

PepsiCo, another giant in the FMCG industry, also offers an attractive average base pay of $68,215 per year for Sales Managers, with an additional yearly pay of $10,203 on average. As a Sales Manager in such a reputable company, you can rest assured of a decent salary package recognizing your hard work and dedication.

43 https://www.indeed.com/career/sales-manager/salaries

CHAPTER 26

WHAT MAKES A STELLAR FMCG SALES TEAM?

As a Sales Manager, you have the exciting opportunity to lead a team and drive success. While you do not need to micromanage, it is crucial to supervise and motivate your team to perform at their best. By embodying these key traits, you can take your FMCG sales team from average to exceptional.

1 – RIGOROUS TRAINING

To maximize your sales potential, having a salesforce that is well-trained, confident, positive, and passionate about their work is crucial. They should possess excellent listening skills, multitask, and consistently develop innovative ideas.

In addition, your team needs to stay up-to-date with the latest sales technology and trends to stay ahead of the competition. This includes training in cloud-based tools and software such as Bitrix24[44], which can be used for effective lead generation.

To excel in their roles, your sales agents must be equipped to handle even the most demanding customers and respond effectively to queries. This can be achieved by providing them with scripts for common objections and having them practice regularly with corporate trainers. With a confident and competent salesforce, you can boost your sales and achieve success in your business.

---

44 https://www.bitrix24.com/

2 – REGULAR COMMUNICATION

To build a highly successful sales team, it is crucial to maintain regular communication with every member. However, you might find it challenging to have individual conversations with each team member. In such a scenario, you can rely on your Account Manager to communicate effectively on your behalf.

Your Account Manager will update you on your team's performance, providing valuable insights into their progress. You should discuss with your Account Manager the quality of your team's performance and feedback to identify areas of improvement and capitalize on their strengths.

Think of your Account Manager as the captain of a championship-winning sports team. A great captain analyzes the team's strengths and weaknesses and makes informed decisions based on the situation. Similarly, a skilled Account Manager leverages customer data to uncover insights about your customers' profiles. This information is then effectively communicated to your salesforce to build lasting relationships with your customers and gain their trust. You can build a team that delivers exceptional results with a confident approach.

3 – TRUST

Trust is an indispensable trait that lays the foundation for building a highly successful sales team. Establishing trust is a challenging task, but breaking it is much easier. When team members trust one another, they can set aside differences, handle conflicts professionally and amicably, and hold each other accountable for the team's success. However, if there is a lack of trust among team members, it becomes difficult for them to succeed. In such cases, conflicts remain unresolved, accountability is compromised, and the overall growth and success of the team is hindered.

4 – COMPLETE PREPAREDNESS

To achieve success in sales, your team needs to have a sales playbook that outlines your sales process, customer profiles, scripts for queries, sample emails, and agendas. Additionally, it can include proposal guidelines, negotiation questions, tips for conducting demos, and more. Your team's Content Writer will play a pivotal role in this process by providing your salesforce with key transcripts and templates. This will empower them to handle demanding customers and easily navigate specific objections, ultimately leading to more successful sales outcomes.

KEY TAKEAWAY

With the right players on your sales team who possess these essential four traits - well-trained, effective communicators, trustworthy, and always prepared - you can confidently take your sales team from good to outstanding.

CHAPTER 27

TRAINING ORDER BOOKERS

In the sales department of an FMCG company, an Order Booker is not just a vital resource but also a key player in the success of your business. The Order Booker is the team member who interacts with customers frequently and, thus, has the power to influence a customer's decision in your favor.

Your organization's order booker will be responsible for receiving and processing incoming orders for goods from retail stores. With their in-depth understanding of customer needs, they can come up with the most effective solutions to satisfy customer demand.

The order booker will receive orders through various channels such as in-person visits, phone calls, emails, or other electronic mediums. Their primary duties include informing customers of prices, receipts, order fulfillment dates, any expected delays, and handling customer complaints. Their customer-centric approach ensures that the customer is satisfied with every aspect of the order process.

To ensure that your order bookers can perform their duties effectively, they must develop several skills. These skills include:

Active Listening – A skilled order booker should be able to actively listen to the customer's needs and requirements without interrupting them at inappropriate times. They should be able to comprehend the conveyed information and ask relevant questions to clarify any doubts or uncertainties. This level of attentiveness and understanding is crucial to providing a confident and satisfactory customer service experience.

Speaking with Conviction – Your order booker must talk with unwavering confidence to convey information to the customers effectively.

Persuasion – In the FMCG industry, countless products share similar features and benefits. That is why your order booker must have the skill to persuade and educate customers on what sets your product apart from the rest. They must clearly demonstrate why customers should choose your product over the competition and why they should stock it on their store shelves. With a confident and informed order booker, you can effectively differentiate your product and drive sales.

Critical Thinking – Order bookers must effectively utilize logic and reasoning when evaluating alternative solutions, conclusions, and approaches to complex problems. Such skills enable them to identify the strengths and weaknesses of each option, ultimately leading to the selection of the most optimal solution.

Time Management – As an order booker, visiting multiple retailers is integral to the daily work routine. Therefore, effective time management skills are crucial to cover more outlets and engage with more retailers.

Social Perceptiveness – It is crucial for order bookers to possess a high degree of social perceptiveness. They should be able to accurately assess the retailers' reactions and understand and address their underlying reasons.

Coordination – Order bookers must be able to adapt their actions based on the actions of others.

INTERVIEW QUESTIONS FOR ORDER BOOKERS

Recruiting the right people for the role of order bookers is crucial to ensuring effective training. It all starts with hiring individuals with the right attitude. Remember, the mantra "Hire for attitude, train for skill" is as relevant for order bookers as any other role in your organization.

To identify the best candidates for the position, asking the right questions during recruitment is crucial. Based on their responses, you will be able to determine which candidates have the potential to succeed as order bookers.

Allow me to share some interview questions that can provide a deeper understanding of the skills and abilities needed and show-case the candidate's competence and suitability.

1. Can you tell me when you dealt with a difficult person and how you handled the situation?

2. Share an example where you demonstrated excellent listening skills?

3. Can you provide an example of when you collected information from several sources?

4. Have you ever gone above and beyond the "call of duty?" (The best answer will show that the candidate is reliable and dependable)

5. Have you ever experienced a situation where you had to compromise on your ethics?

6. Can you share an example of when you overcame obstacles?

7. Do you have experience preparing invoices, shipping contracts, or other documents?

8. How do you maintain a balance between cooperating with others and independent thinking? (Try to establish if the candidate can work cooperatively with others and has a good nature)

9. Tell me about a time when you resolved a problematic customer complaint?

10. Share an experience where someone tested your patience. How were you able to keep your emotions in check?

11. Can you share an effective technique you used to sell customers additional services or merchandise?

12. Have you ever computed total service, merchandise, and/or shipping charges?

13. What tools and techniques do you need to keep inventory records up to date?

14. Describe an experience where you had to work with difficult people to help your employer or company? (Make sure the candidate has strong negotiation skills)

15. Can you provide a time when you could identify a complex problem and implement a solution?

For more interview questions for order bookers, visit Job Interview Questions[45].

KEY TAKEAWAY

Order bookers are an integral part of your sales team, and their role in building and generating revenue for your organization cannot be overstated. By implementing effective recruitment strategies and investing in skills development, you can ensure that your order bookers add maximum value to your organization. So,

---

45 https://www.jobinterviewquestions.com/order-clerk/order-booker

follow the best practices outlined above and get the most out of your order bookers.

CHAPTER 28

APPLYING SEGMENTATION TO SALES

S ales segmentation is a powerful strategy that enables companies to create tailored sales approaches that resonate with different types of customers. By analyzing key characteristics such as interests, budgets, and needs, businesses can identify high-potential segments[46] or clusters within their target market and develop highly focused sales strategies to engage and convert them. The advantage of this approach is that it allows organizations to work more efficiently with distinct groups of clients or customers, leading to improved sales performance and overall business success.

HOW TO EFFECTIVELY IMPLEMENT SEGMENTATION IN SALES?

To effectively implement segmentation in sales, it is crucial to have a well-defined set of measurable components that can be closely monitored, analyzed, and adjusted over time to assess the efficacy of your new strategies. These foundational components should be an integral part of your sales process and assist you in making data-driven decisions that drive revenue growth. These basic components include:

Clearly Defined Segments – To maximize the efficiency and effectiveness of your resources, it is essential to identify unique market

---

46 https://www.investopedia.com/terms/m/marketsegmentation.asp

segments and clearly define their attributes or characteristics. By doing so, you can better allocate your time and resources to each segment, ensuring your efforts are tailored to meet their needs and requirements. Remember, every segment should be distinct from the others, and understanding these differences will enable you to navigate each market segment and achieve your goals.

Early Access – When communicating your message, it is essential to factor in your target segment's interests, habits, and resources. This includes considering the popularity of distribution channels, the types of available devices, and internet accessibility. Doing so ensures that your message is delivered effectively to your intended audience.

Business Capacity – To successfully target a market segment, it is crucial to have a thorough understanding of your business's capabilities. It is about finding the ideal segment and ensuring you have the necessary production capacity, budget, and resources to handle the demand. You can identify and target the most lucrative market segments by carefully assessing your business's capacity.

Relevance and Size – Based on my experience, calculating the size of a specific segment is crucial in determining the conversion potential. It helps evaluate the profitability of customized marketing techniques and ensures that the revenue gained is well worth the expense.

Market segmentation is crucial for any business looking to thrive in the competitive market. Fortunately, several online tools are available to make this process easier and more effective. If you are looking for a tool that can help you with both quantitative and qualitative segmentation, upBOARD's Online Market Segmentation Tools[47] is a perfect choice. With its user-friendly web

47 https://upboard.io/market-segmentation-online-tools-templates-software/

templates and input forms, you can easily collect, analyze, and report data to gain valuable insights into your target customers and their preferences. So why wait? Start using upBOARD's Online Market Segmentation Tools today and take your business to the next level!

BENEFITS OF APPLYING SEGMENTATION TO SALES

Segmentation in sales offers numerous benefits that can significantly boost your business. Here are some of the key advantages of using segmentation in sales:

1. Improving your product and services – To become a company that provides the best solutions, knowing WHO is interested in purchasing WHAT and WHY is crucial. You can position yourself as the go-to solution provider when you clearly understand your customer's preferences and needs. Your ability to meet your customer's needs will increase their satisfaction and give you an edge over your competitors.

2. Generating Higher Revenues – Investing your time and efforts in the wrong customer segments can lead to a considerable waste of resources. The wrong segment may have a lower upsell potential or a higher churn rate after the initial purchase, leading to a decrease in revenue and customer base instability. By using segmentation, you can confidently identify and target the right segments, which will boost your revenues and ensure the stability of your customer base.

3. Increases Sales – As a part of the sales team, your ultimate goal is to increase sales, and with the correct customer segmentation, you can definitely achieve it! It is important to note that losing a few customers along the way is inevitable when filtering your customer base. However, with the right strategy, you can become your market leader and successfully steal customers from your competitors. Remember, you have the tools and skills to achieve your sales goals and dominate your industry.

4. Emphasize Your Marketing Communication – Conducting customer segmentation is crucial to enhance your product. This will aid in developing a more customized marketing message designed to target each of your top segments and increase interest in your product. By focusing on your best segments, you can create a tailored marketing approach guaranteed to succeed.

After analyzing your customer base, you will better understand its distinctive groups and their specific requirements. Armed with this knowledge, you can segment your customers and cater to their unique needs more effectively.

KEY TAKEAWAY

Segmentation is a powerful tool that can help your sales team close more deals by enabling them to convert prospects into customers easily. By leveraging your marketing campaigns to attract customers most suited to your business's offerings, you can identify the segments that need your product the most. Armed with this knowledge, your sales team can confidently engage with potential customers and close deals quickly and efficiently.

In addition, segmentation can help your sales force develop more compelling sales pitches and marketing campaigns by pinpointing your product's unique selling proposition (USP). This allows them to differentiate your product and make it more appealing to your target market, resulting in increased sales and a more robust bottom line.

CHAPTER 29

SALES IN MODERN TRADE

Let us begin by understanding what modern trade entails. It is a highly organized and structured logistics and distribution management approach involving major players such as hypermarkets and supermarket chains. This approach includes demand aggregation across diverse products, making it a highly efficient and effective sales method. With its well-established processes and systems, modern trade offers a reliable and trustworthy platform for businesses to expand their reach and maximize their sales potential.

Modern retailers today are effective in their inventory management strategies. They maintain inventory levels well above their safety stock, ensuring enough supply to meet immediate demand. Delivery windows are a top priority for retailers, with specific timeslots dedicated for each product replenishment. Retailers are known to hold distributors accountable for delays or missed delivery timeslots, reinforcing the efficiency of their well-defined inventory and delivery processes.

MERCHANDISING

In today's highly competitive FMCG market, where modern trade is replacing traditional trade, it is imperative for sales teams to proactively establish their presence in modern trade outlets to stay ahead of the competition.

With the right merchandising strategy, the sales and merchandising teams can significantly enhance the visibility of your product and drive sales. Follow these steps to ensure a successful merchandising solution.

Tracking Attendance – You should be able to monitor the attendance of your merchandising team and ensure that it is going as per the journey plan.

Ensure Delivery – The delivery to modern trade outlets should be verified to ensure that it has been made in strict compliance with the purchase order issued.

Check Primary Axis Point – To accurately assess the performance of a product, it is essential to measure a variety of metrics, including the number of SKUs, the share of shelf, the share of shelf for all competitor products, the freshness of the products in question, and metrics against minimum bare quantity. Analyzing these metrics, you can comprehensively understand the product's success and make informed decisions.

Check Secondary Axis Point – You can ensure an all-inclusive analysis by thoroughly inspecting all secondary axis points, including point of sales units, bins, gondolas, end caps, and more.

Check Tertiary Axis Point – Checking the available stock in the backdoor, your sales and merchandising teams can ensure they are always equipped to fulfill orders immediately, even if the stock is running low. This ensures that you can deliver the best possible service to our customers.

POINT-OF-SALES TOOLS

At a retail outlet, visual merchandising or point-of-sales material (POSM) tools are crucial in creating a positive image of your product and influencing your current and prospective customers' attention, interest, desire, and action. All the tools used should contribute to sales, brand building, and the product's image. In short, having a well-crafted visual merchandising strategy can significantly boost your business and help you stand out.

Point-of-sale materials and tools are crucial for businesses looking to boost sales and attract customers. By incorporating the right visual merchandising elements, you can effectively maintain the overall brand image in your customers' minds and influence their decision to purchase. In modern trade, these visual merchandising elements generally fall into the following categories:

Posters/Danglers – Eliminating clutter from sales counters and floors is crucial. However, posters and banners can communicate your product's message effectively, creating a powerful visual impact. These cost-effective and attractive marketing tools are easily placeable in modern trade outlets, making them an ideal solution for boosting sales and achieving your marketing goals.

End Cap – The end cap placement shelf, positioned at the end of an aisle in a modern trade outlet, is widely acknowledged as the most effective way to attract customers and gain an edge over your competition. When you use an end cap, you aim to highlight your preferred products or new launches, resulting in increased impulse purchases. So, an end cap placement is an excellent strategy to boost sales and grow your brand's visibility.

In-Store Branding– To successfully sell your products, creating a visually appealing environment that embodies your brand is crucial.

Strategically placing prints and creatives on pillars, walls, glass, and floors is an effective way to achieve this. When it comes to in-shop branding, these tools are widely accepted and have been proven to increase customer engagement and sales.

Pillar/Wall branding - The walls and pillars are adorned with printed graphics to capture the attention of potential customers.

Glass branding - Vinyl prints offer a versatile solution for branding on entrances/windows or partitions. By highlighting ongoing offers and discounts, branding on glass can effectively attract footfall and increase business. You can trust in the power of these branding techniques to make an impact on your customers.

Vendor Shops - Vendor shops are an excellent way for FMCG companies to stand out in retail stores. By creating a "store within a store" or "shop-in-shop," vendors can showcase their products uniquely and eye-catching, drawing attention to their brand and increasing sales. This approach is instrumental when competing for limited shelf space in stores. Compared to traditional product placement on shelves, vendor shops create a more sophisticated and elaborate display that can significantly impact consumer behavior.

CHAPTER 30

SELLING TO MOM-AND-POP STORES

S mall, family-owned independent stores that sell a limited range of products, including FMCG products, are known as mom-and-pop stores. While these stores face competition from larger establishments such as Carrefour, Wal-Mart, Target, etc., that have more buying power, statistics show that mom-and-pop stores still represent a significant share of retail sales in Latin America and other emerging markets. In fact, they are expected to continue to do so for a long time. Therefore, it is safe to say that mom-and-pop stores are still a force to be reckoned with in the retail industry.

Large packaged-good companies have long enjoyed robust profit margins by selling their products directly to small, independent stores. These mom-and-pop retailers typically have little bargaining power and often agree to provide favorable distribution deals in exchange for additional support, such as shelving, display refrigerators, freezers, grab-and-go coolers, and other merchandising services.

FMCG companies can no longer rely on earning easy profits from mom-and-pop stores. The increasing number of consumer goods companies and brands vying for limited cash and shelf space has become challenging. However, companies willing to adapt to the changing market conditions can still succeed by leveraging innovative strategies and differentiated products.

To maintain profitable relationships with mom-and-pop stores and to overcome competition in this challenging channel, it is crucial to acknowledge a reality that has been ignored for a long time. Mom-and-pop stores are incredibly diverse, and the same customers visit different ones throughout the week on various occasions, even though these stores are located close to one another and often stock the same products. By embracing this reality, you can confidently navigate the complexities of this market and stay ahead of your competition.

To fully capitalize on the diverse range of outlets available, it is essential to segment them in the same manner as experienced sales and marketing professionals segment consumers. This involves an in-depth understanding of the various occasions when different individuals are more likely to shop at certain stores. Additionally, you must identify the factors that appeal to these customers when they shop and why different store owners are loyal to particular suppliers. By doing so, you can gain a competitive advantage and make smarter business decisions.

After thoroughly grasping the mentioned points, you can identify the shops that deserve investment and create compelling displays, discounts, incentives, sales, and distribution plans to significantly enhance your sales and provide financial benefits to shop owners.

MERCHANDISING

Effective merchandising is crucial for the success of any product, but it is even more critical for mom-and-pop stores. With limited space available, it is essential to strategically place your products in a way that catches the attention of potential customers. Even if you have the best inventory, it will not matter if it is not easily visible and accessible to shoppers. As a merchandiser or stockist, you hold the key to the success of your product in the store, and excellent retail merchandising can make all the difference. So be strategic in your approach to merchandising, and watch your sales soar!

Proper layout and visibility are crucial for driving sales and gaining an edge over competitors. Your merchandisers can significantly impact sales by ensuring proper visual merchandising in mom-and-pop stores. By strategically placing your product in a prominent position that catches the customer's eye, you can entice them to buy more of your product and gain an advantage over your rivals. Remember, a little effort towards visual merchandising can go a long way in boosting sales and generating greater profits.

Ideally, a separate merchandising team should be created for FMCG sales companies to ensure maximum sales and customer satisfaction. The team would be responsible for:

- Providing effective point-of-purchase and shelf management services.
- Maintaining strong customer relationships.
- Responding to customer inquiries while highlighting the features of company products.
- Ensuring that store shelves are always stocked with the correct inventory.
- Removing damaged or expired products.
- Maintaining an optimum display of products.
- Providing support to field sales representatives with special promotions, effectively setting up displays, and checking on special promotions daily.
- Reporting customer feedback to management.

- Enforcing standards and taking ownership of the job.

- Enhancing the organization's reputation and exploring opportunities to add value to their accomplishments.

POINT-OF-SALES TOOLS

Based on the above discussion, I can confidently say that mom-and-pop stores face intense competition due to the abundance of FMCG products available in the market. However, you can leverage innovative point-of-sale tools to help these stores stand out. Here are some practical tools that we can use:

Freestanding Displays - Freestanding displays are a great way to showcase a specific product and grab customers' attention. These displays are made from cardboard, allowing you to customize them according to your preferences and the store's overall look and feel. With freestanding displays, you can promote your products and create an impactful visual display that draws customers in.

Dump Bins - Dump bins are the perfect standalone displays for retailers who want to showcase their products in a unique and eye-catching way. These displays are larger than freestanding displays and ideal for displaying small, individually packaged goods such as candy. With dump bins, you can be sure customers will notice your products.

Banner Stands - Banner stands are an excellent form of standalone signage that can be easily placed throughout a store. Although larger than most POSM tools, they are highly portable, allowing store owners to position them wherever they want. Unlike other POSM tools, banner stands only act as advertising and signage, making them effective for promoting products or services.

CHAPTER 31

DIFFERENTIATING FROM COMPETITORS

C reating a product that stands out from the competition is crucial to generating sales in the highly saturated FMCG industry. Fortunately, several effective ways exist to differentiate your product and increase consumer appeal.

PACKAGING DIFFERENTIATION

Packaging has emerged as a savior amid the vast array of FMCG products. Packaging differentiation draws attention by setting a brand apart in numerous ways. Sales professionals are well aware of this fact, which is why brands are now undergoing packaging refreshment initiatives more often than ever before. Unique and imaginative packaging can help you define your brand, making it more meaningful and attracting the necessary attention that drives sales.

BRANDING DIFFERENTIATION

When it comes to branding, it is essential to remember that customers view brands as people. Even common household goods have a unique personality that sets them apart from the competition. As a brand, your goal should be establishing a robust and lasting relationship with your consumers, surpassing your rivals. To achieve this, you must understand your customers' likes, preferences, and who they want to interact with. You can create a powerful connection with your audience by speaking to them in their language and using branding colors, logos, and fonts that they find visually appealing. With the right taglines and advertisements, you can leave an iconic impression on your customers that will keep them returning for more.

Building a solid brand requires consistent messaging across all platforms, including social media. Maintaining a distinctive brand voice in every post and comment you make is crucial, as it helps your followers connect with you on a deeper level. You become the go-to brand in their minds by creating a strong and lasting relationship with your audience. Even if they come across similar products from your competitors, your loyal customers will always choose you first. A consistent brand voice can make all the difference in building a lasting and successful business.

VALUE DIFFERENTIATION

If you have the same products as your competitors, do not worry. You can still stand out by offering something unique. One way to do this is by providing a wider range of options. Consider selling additional products or upselling existing ones your competition currently does not offer. You can even retail products from other brands that your customers like. By doing so, you will become a one-stop shop for all their related needs, making their lives much easier. Offering convenience and value will help you differentiate your brand and boost sales.

POINT-OF-SALES TOOLS DIFFERENTIATION

By now, you must be convinced that point-of-sales tools can work wonders for your business. To truly stand out from the competition, you need to get creative with your displays. Here are some unique and eye-catching ideas that will help you break through the clutter and ensure your brand is the one that customers remember.

LED Displays at Checkout Counters – LED lights bring a new level of sophistication and elegance to the traditional unlit displays. From in-store marketing to self-service checkouts and price-checks, LED displays are the ideal choice. They offer unmatched versatility, reliability, and style, making them the ultimate upgrade for any business looking to make a bold statement.

KEY TAKEAWAY

FMCG businesses must continually adapt to outperform their competitors to thrive in today's rapidly changing retail environment. This means having a deep understanding of how to effectively differentiate products at the point of sale, where customers make critical purchasing decisions. Whether stocking your goods in traditional mom-and-pop shops or modern trade outlets, implementing these proven differentiation techniques can give your business a significant sales boost all year round. With the right strategy and mindset, you can navigate the ever-evolving retail landscape and achieve long-term success.

CHAPTER 32

BRAINSTORMING UNIQUE SALES ACTIVATION PROGRAMS

A s a sales professional, you have the expertise and drive to expand your customer base continuously. The market can indeed be quite competitive, but you know that your product stands out from the rest. You can break through the clutter and win over potential customers with your unwavering ability to showcase the unique features and benefits.

A sales activation program can be the most effective solution for such situations. This chapter will delve into the definition of sales activation programs and provide some actionable ideas to help you establish stronger customer connections. But before we get into that, let us take a closer look at what sales activation means.

WHAT IS SALES ACTIVATION?

Sales activation, also known as conversion, is the moment of truth when a prospective customer decides to purchase. It typically occurs at the bottom of the sales funnel, during the decision-making phase, when the customer evaluates their options and determines whether your product meets their needs. At this crucial stage, you must instill confidence in your potential customers and demonstrate how your product can provide the value they seek.

You must focus on sales activation efforts to generate sales and drive revenue. These marketing campaigns are specifically designed to target in-market buyers actively seeking to solve their problems.

By directing your efforts towards this audience, you can attract people who are most likely to buy your product or service and increase your chances of success. That is why sales activation objectives should be a top priority for any business looking to boost its sales and grow its bottom line.

It is crucial to implement a comprehensive sales activation campaign to drive sales. This can include tactics such as running highly targeted Google Search Ads aimed at bottom-of-funnel search terms, leveraging search engine optimization (SEO) to rank for buyer-intent keywords, and utilizing Facebook retargeting to bring prospects back to an abandoned shopping cart. However, do not be afraid to think big and organize elaborate events to showcase your products. By implementing a well-rounded sales activation strategy, you will boost your visibility and persuade buyers to choose your product over competitors.

Based on actual success stories, here are some creative sales activation ideas that can help you effectively engage with your target audience and achieve your marketing goals.

PROMOTE UNIQUE CUSTOMER EXPERIENCES - CONTOURS

Creating a remarkable customer experience requires a touch of ingenuity, something that will leave a lasting impression on your audience. Contours' Baby Stroller Test Ride is a brilliant illustration of this. The company developed adult-sized strollers that allow parents to experience the product's quality firsthand. How many people can brag about riding in a stroller as an adult? Not many, which is precisely what makes this sales activation exceptional and unrivaled.

SOLVE CUSTOMER PROBLEMS – VITAMIN WATER

To understand why people buy things, you must dive deeper and realize that every purchase solves a problem. As a business, your goal should be to identify your target audience's challenges and offer solutions that can help them. Vitaminwater[48], for instance, came up with a brilliant idea to promote its brand at the WayHome Music Festival - a human car wash that helped festival-goers beat the summer heat. Vitaminwater solved a common problem and increased awareness of its product by providing a fun misting station.

LEVERAGE CURRENT TRENDS – INNOCENT DRINKS

Innocent Drinks' sales activation program is one of the most innovative on my list. By opening a popup bar with only one way to order – share a picture on social media and tag it with the brand's unique emoji hashtag – Innocent Drinks creatively created awareness of their product. Through this campaign, they cleverly capitalized on the emoji trend, capturing the attention of millennials with their tiki-themed "Coconut Watering Hole" and successfully promoting their products.

KEY TAKEAWAY

To achieve success in any sales activation program, it is vital to have a comprehensive approach. The key takeaways include:

1. **Focusing on your audience** and delivering value to them.

2. **Ensure your experiences are shareable,** making it easier for customers to share their positive experiences on social media.

---

48 https://robyncambruzzi.com/portfolio/vitaminwater-hydration-station/

3. **Aim for excellence** by differentiating yourself from your competitors.

Even if your sales activation program is imperfect, it should provide unique and unforgettable experiences that keep your customers returning for more.

CHAPTER 33

IMPORTANCE OF PRODUCT LAUNCHES IN FMCG SALES

To ensure the success of any FMCG product in the market, it is indispensable to have a robust product launch. Top-performing sales professionals agree that, among all the stages involved in product development, launching is the most crucial one that can either make or break the entire process. The significance of a product launch is so immense that many FMCG companies appoint a dedicated team of experts to ensure its success. Let us look at some of the benefits of a product launch.

COMPANY AND PRODUCT ATTENTION

A successful product launch is a powerful tool to bring attention to your company. A well-crafted press release can attract readers, create awareness about your new product, and introduce your company to potential customers. As readers engage with the story online, they will likely visit your website to learn more about the product, resulting in increased sales and a more extensive customer base. A product launch can be a game-changer for your business with the right approach.

BUILDS YOUR COMPANY'S REPUTATION

When you successfully launch a product that sells well or fulfills an unmet need in the market - especially one that other companies have overlooked - your business has the potential to become a dominant player in the industry. You can establish a reputation as an industry leader by developing game-changing products and bringing them to market. This, in turn, earns your target audience's trust, making it more likely that your next product launch will be a resounding success, thanks to your track record of creating innovative products and building a solid brand reputation.

CAPTURE MARKET SHARE

You can dominate the market by introducing a new product, even if similar products are already available. The novelty and excitement of your product can capture people's attention and attract first-time buyers. By converting these buyers into loyal customers, you can increase your market share and establish yourself as a major player in the industry.

KEY TAKEAWAY

A successful product launch can gain customers, enhance your company's reputation, and establish new business relationships and partnerships. Your new product can attract investment from more prominent FMCG firms or help you sell to a larger audience in a revenue-sharing model. So, be confident in your product, plan well, and execute flawlessly to maximize this opportunity.

CHAPTER 34

BUSINESS ANALYTICS IN SALES

Tracking sales data across all variables, such as customers, pricing, and products, is the key to success in today's hyper-competitive FMCG world. Business analytics in sales can help your company stand out among others fighting for the same market share. With the ability to track what customers are buying, what products are trending down, and what stores or sales areas are struggling, you can gain actionable intelligence. This intelligence can be used to position your company for growth better and prevent challenges before they impact your bottom line. So, unleash the power of business analytics to enhance your sales efforts and propel your business to new heights of success.

Here are some effective ways to leverage analytics to boost your sales performance:

1. SELL MORE TO CURRENT CUSTOMERS

As we have established in the previous chapters, retaining existing customers is much more cost-effective than acquiring new ones. In fact, according to a study by Parature, selling to an existing customer is up to fourteen times more likely than selling to a new one. By utilizing business analytics, your sales team can better understand your customers' purchasing habits, including what they are and are not buying. This valuable information allows you to identify demand trends and pinpoint opportunities for cross-selling. For example, if one of your customers buys shampoo but not conditioner, you can launch a targeted campaign to promote conditioner to that customer. With such insights, you can confidently make data-driven decisions that drive your business forward.

2. IDENTIFY BEST-SELLING PRODUCTS

As an FMCG company, you have a wide range of products to offer, but identifying the ones performing well, contributing to other sales, or even those on the decline is a complex task. However, analyzing trends in product sales from past transactions can help you identify when a product is on the rise or rapidly declining.

By doing so, you can spot inconsistencies in profit margins or changes in the quantities sold due to competition. With this information, you can adjust your sales strategy accordingly and drive your business toward success.

3. MAKE DATA-DRIVEN DECISIONS

To outperform your competitors and stay ahead of the curve, you must have consistent access to your company's data and leverage it to make informed decisions. Relying on intuition or emotional decisions can lead to risks you cannot afford to take.

By breaking down sales data into product, customer, or sales rep categories, you can approach performance reviews with insights that enable each rep to achieve higher sales or restore broken customer relationships. By having detailed information about historical product sales across various industries, you can ensure that your team is ready to handle spikes in demand and answer any customer queries that may arise. These are just two examples of how you can make more data-driven decisions.

With accurate and timely data, you can easily justify your actions with your team and customers. So, embrace data as a powerful tool to help you make informed decisions to drive your business toward success.

4. PROMOTES PRODUCT DEVELOPMENT

To remain competitive in a customer-centric market, your product must be tailored to meet your customer's needs. You can effectively determine what works and what does not by conducting surveys or performing A/B testing to experiment with different approaches. Utilizing customer feedback can be a powerful tool to improve the quality of your product or service levels and identify opportunities for innovation that will set you apart from the competition. With this information, you can make decisions to drive your business forward.

5. OPTIMIZE YOUR PRICING STRUCTURE

By leveraging the power of business analytics, you can master the art of pricing your products competitively. With access to critical financials for each product line, including costs, revenue, and quantities, you can define the best value price for your business and your customers. Plus, with the ability to track these price changes, you can make informed decisions that positively impact your bottom line. Trust in the power of data and take control of your pricing strategy today.

6. CREATE COHERENCE BETWEEN DEPARTMENTS

Actionable intelligence is a game-changer for your business. It is not just your sales team who will benefit from knowing what products are selling and to whom. Every area of your business can become more efficient by using this knowledge. Operations can plan and forecast product demand more accurately, translating to better preparation for manufacturing, product development, and customer service. Marketing can identify which campaigns drive sales and refine those that are not. Management can access high-level details about sales activity through executive dashboards, empowering them to make strategic decisions for the company's benefit and justify future investments in sales. With a single source of truth for data, value is created between departments and across the business.

KEY TAKEAWAY

As a sales leader, staying on top of various key performance indicators, ranging from individual and team performance to inventory, marketing campaigns, and product sales, is crucial. With Intelex Business Management Software[49] and DBxtra[50], you can efficiently manage all these data points from one place and keep your analytics up-to-date.

These business intelligence tools empower you to approach every interaction with your sales team fully informed about their territories and customers. You can address concerns and communicate progress while providing them with meaningful scorecards, valuable data, and overall views of everything they need to address with customers.

Remember, sales is the driving force behind any business's growth, and improving your sales team's effectiveness should always be your top priority. You can lead your team and succeed with the right tools and data.

---

49 https://www.intelex.com/products/applications/
50 https://dbxtra.com/

CHAPTER 35

PREDICTING SALES USING BUSINESS ANALYTICS

B y utilizing statistical models and computer algorithms, business analytics helps analyze large datasets to determine the probability of a set of possible outcomes. Using current, historical, and contextual data, these models can predict the likelihood of future events.

Sales teams increasingly rely on business analytics to examine past behaviors of leads and customers and identify patterns that can help them identify profitable prospects. It is important to note that predictive analytics in sales differs from marketing analytics, which primarily focuses on creating demand instead of generating revenue. If you are looking to leverage business analytics in sales, here are some practical ways to do so.

1. HELP YOUR SALES TEAM PRIORITIZE LEADS AND ACCOUNTS

Determining KPIs is crucial for steering your sales team in the right direction. By focusing on the individuals and accounts with a higher probability of conversion and retention, you can optimize your sales resources and improve customer lifetime value. Business analytics is a powerful tool that:

- Empowers you to prioritize leads based on their likelihood to act and purchase.

- Helps you segment leads and tailor marketing messages to their specific needs, giving you a competitive edge in the market.

To truly reap the benefits of lead prioritization and qualification, it is imperative to have ample customer data at your disposal. The more data you have, the more comprehensive your decision-making process can become, ultimately leading to better results. To take your lead qualification process to the next level, consider utilizing powerful business analytics tools like Pathmonk[51].

2. MODEL AND PREDICT CUSTOMER DATA

By utilizing machine learning algorithms on your customer data, you gain the ability to predict and anticipate your customer's next move in a way that "reads your customer's mind." This allows you to offer products or services they may need and provides a more personalized and proactive customer service experience. With this approach, you can stay ahead of the competition by staying one step ahead of your customers and meeting their needs before they even realize it.

KEY TAKEAWAY

With the ever-increasing role of big data and AI-powered predictive sales software, you can now use cutting-edge technology to predict and respond to customer behavior. Once you have the right tools in place, you can effectively target the right customers at the right time, deliver personalized sales and marketing communications, and achieve the most significant impact possible. By leveraging predictive analytics, you can spend less time speculating and more time transforming profitable leads and enhancing your customer lifetime value.

51 https://pathmonk.com/lead-qualification-tool/

CHAPTER 36

CASE STUDY OF A LEADING FMCG COMPANY

This chapter will examine the practical aspects of FMCG sales and explore what occurs in the real world, taking a step away from the theoretical realm.

This case study will explore how mobile media's power can be harnessed to generate valuable insights and boost sales for FMCG brands. Our focus company is none other than Unilever, a global giant in the FMCG industry that supplies personal care, home, and food products. With an impressive portfolio of world-renowned and well-loved brands, Unilever is a force to be reckoned with.

Unilever, the FMCG powerhouse, has a remarkable presence across nearly 100 countries worldwide. The company's annual sales in the UK, the second-biggest market in Unilever's portfolio after the US, amount to a staggering £2.5 billion. It is interesting to note that food brands contribute to over 50% of the company's global sales.

Pot Noodle, a brand launched by Unilever in Britain in 1979, dominates the hot snack market with a staggering 95 percent share, making it the 23rd largest food brand in the country.

Unilever's primary goal was to establish whether a mobile marketing campaign could leverage customer data and boost the sales of Pot Noodles. The company believed mobile phones could provide a more thrilling experience to Pot Noodle customers than traditional channels. Additionally, using mobile phones to offer the prize would simplify and reduce the cost of promotional fulfillment while also allowing for the collection of valuable customer data.

To deliver their solution, Unilever strategically partnered with Flytext, a leading mobile marketing service provider. They also collaborated with Experian, a renowned industry player, to collect and provide valuable customer insights. Leveraging Flytxt's cutting-edge Mobile2Mail service, customers can now easily request brochures, product samples, catalogs, or forms using their mobile phones.

Unilever provided an incredible opportunity to its customers by allowing them to win a Pot Noodle Horn. This was achieved by disclosing a unique winning number in each Pot Noodle pack. Over a million unique winning numbers were available, and customers were urged to text their unique code, name, house number, and postcode. With this information, Flytxt automated matching of the customer's address against the Electoral Roll and Post Office database to ensure the accuracy of the address provided. This made generating a complete address for every customer possible, which Unilever later confirmed.

Through the use of Experian's consumer databases, the address information was enhanced and profiled with various lifestyle and demographic information. This involved analyzing factors such as age, media preferences, and lifestyles and leveraging Experian's Mosaic UK consumer classification. Furthermore, they could identify varying response levels across different parts of the country by logging and scrutinizing the geographical area from which the response originated. With these comprehensive insights, they could make informed decisions based on the data.

Unilever's campaign exceeded expectations, generating an impressive 3,000 daily responses at its peak, coinciding with TV coverage, over four weeks from the end of June to the beginning of July. The campaign resulted in a database of over 190,000 clean and validated customer addresses, surpassing Unilever's goals.

Based on the analysis of responses using Experian's demographic and lifestyle information, it was concluded that Unilever has successfully reached its intended target audience. The analysis also revealed the differences in response rates across towns and cities throughout the country and specific supermarket outlets. The insights gained from this exercise were highly valuable and have been effectively utilized to inform subsequent campaigns, including decisions related to geographic targeting, media selection, and ongoing CRM.

CHAPTER 37

THE POTENTIAL OF E-COMMERCE TO BOOST FMCG SALES

E-commerce provides consumers with the convenience of purchasing products 24/7. It expands a brand's reach and delivers a seamless shopping experience for individual buyers. Furthermore, FMCG e-commerce provides a sense of autonomy, allowing brands to expand their product lines, experiment with innovative tools, and offer various payment options without being constrained by traditional retailer relationships.

Each year, more and more FMCG brands are embracing e-commerce to stay competitive in the market. With each year, more brands are adopting e-commerce, and it's crucial to follow suit. According to Nielsen's recent study, e-commerce is expected to contribute 11 percent of global FMCG sales by 2030, eight times more than the current level. This fact alone makes it evident that your FMCG brand must have a robust e-commerce presence to cater to the expected surge in consumer demand over the next few years. Therefore, it is not just essential but also imperative to have a solid e-commerce strategy in place for your brand.

Your FMCG brand can unlock its true potential by selling products directly to consumers through your e-commerce sites. While you may currently be relying on physical retail outlets, restaurants, or digital retailers like eBay and Amazon, there are six undeniable benefits that e-commerce can offer you. Do not miss out on this incredible opportunity to take your brand to the next level and reach more customers than ever before.

1. GET ACCESS TO CUSTOMER DATA

If you have an e-commerce store, you have a significant advantage of collecting valuable consumer data. With this data, you can gain insights into your consumer's buying behavior and establish a direct relationship with them. Analyzing your consumer's purchasing patterns and best-selling products becomes easier once you collect all the data. This puts you in a better position to make informed decisions and grow your business.

Utilizing your data's insights can significantly enhance customers' online shopping experience. It is imperative to be transparent with them and communicate how their data will be used. This not only helps to establish trust and loyalty but also improves the overall customer experience.

2. PERSONALIZATION

In the world of e-commerce, there is no doubt that Amazon stands as the undisputed leader when it comes to offering a personalized shopping experience to its customers. From start to finish, Amazon's end-to-end personalization ensures a seamless and hassle-free purchase every single time. By leveraging the power of marketing personalization, you can reap numerous benefits, such as increased customer advocacy, stronger relationships with your existing customer base, and even attracting new customers to your business.

3. GET AN EDGE OVER COMPETITION

With the anticipated growth of FMCG sales in e-commerce to continue, now is the perfect opportunity to gain a competitive edge and stand out from your FMCG rivals by selling your products on your e-commerce platform. This move will not only help your brand take center stage in the digital space but also enable you to provide attractive incentives for customers to visit your e-commerce store. Do not settle for a plain, boring site with irrelevant information. Instead, make the most of this opportunity to showcase your products and brand and capture a significant online market share.

4. BOOST REPEAT PURCHASES

Your customers will always come back to your e-commerce store if they are satisfied with the service and products they receive from you. According to a survey by Yotpo[52], a leading e-commerce marketing platform, exceptional customer service makes 39% of shoppers loyal to their favorite brands. Therefore, e-commerce functionality on your FMCG site is essential to boost consumer loyalty and ensure repeat purchases.

When customers think positively of your brand, they will visit your site to search for your products and expect to find and buy them easily and quickly. This is where repeat purchases and consumer loyalty come into play. Consistently providing an amazing experience to your customers will make them return to your site repeatedly.

Online reviews are crucial in building customer trust, and as many as 84% of people trust them as much as personal recommendations. This means that repeat purchases and consumer advocacy will

52 https://www.yotpo.com/

contribute significantly to the growth of your brand. Moreover, increasing per customer and frequency of purchasing will prove to be a highly cost-effective technique to attract new customers.

5. FREE OF COMPETITIVE CLUTTER

In the fiercely competitive retail world, capturing a consumer's attention amidst a sea of other brands vying for their share of the wallet can be pretty challenging. However, with an e-commerce site, you can gain a significant advantage over your competitors. People who visit your online store have already expressed an interest in your products and are actively seeking to fulfill a need. This means you have a captive audience free from distractions or clutter from other brands. With complete control over your brand platform, you can create an exceptional user experience, tailor-made promotions, and brand messaging that resonates with your audience. By leveraging the benefits of e-commerce, you can effectively maximize engagement, boost your sales, and establish your brand as a force to be reckoned with in the marketplace.

6. NO INTERFERENCE FROM RETAILERS

Online shopping is rapidly transforming the retail industry, and FMCG brands looking to shift from conventional retailers to online marketplaces like Amazon must be aware of the potential restrictions they may face. When you rely on third-party retailers to sell your products, you lose control over how you market your brand and may even lose out on expensive profit margins to retail giants who dictate the terms.

However, with your e-commerce site, your FMCG brand can break free from the limitations set by third-party retailers and take complete control of your marketing strategy. You will be able to retain a significant portion of your profits and be free to execute your ideas how you want. According to a report by Forbes, 19 percent of consumers prefer to purchase products directly from brands, while only 12 percent would choose to buy from online marketplaces such as Amazon.

KEY TAKEAWAY

If you want to expand your sales revenue and maintain brand ownership, establishing your e-commerce website is a critical step you cannot overlook.

CHAPTER 38

KEEPING UP WITH E-COMMERCE

The COVID-19 pandemic has caused a significant increase in e-commerce, making it a booming industry. Every day, more and more retailers move their business online while entrepreneurs kickstart their e-commerce ventures. According to Forbes Advisor, worldwide revenues from e-commerce are expected to reach $6.31 trillion by the end of 2023, which is a notable increase of 10.4% compared to 2022. Moreover, it is projected to reach $8.148 trillion by 2026.

E-commerce is a dynamic industry that evolves rapidly. Every year, new trends emerge that can help your FMCG business grow and surpass your competitors. As part of an FMCG sales team, staying on top of these emerging trends and adopting them as soon as possible is crucial. Here are the top four trends you need to watch out for.

1. VOICE COMMERCE IS GOING TO INCREASE

Voice assistant devices like Google Home with Google Assistant and Amazon Echo with Alexa are rapidly gaining popularity, and for good reason. They offer convenience and ease of use, allowing people to do everything from turning on the lights to purchasing products online with just their voice. With nearly 75 percent of households in the US expected to have smart speakers by 2025, and according to Statista, voice commerce sales are predicted to grow fourfold by 2023 versus 2021 to reach $20 billion, it is clear that this trend is here to stay.

Thanks to technological advancements, virtual assistants are becoming more accurate and capable of understanding regional languages, making voice commerce even more accessible to users. As a result, optimizing your e-commerce store for voice search is no longer just an option but a strategic necessity. By embracing this trend, you can stay ahead of the competition and provide an exceptional customer experience that will keep your business thriving.

Voice commerce has become a major digital player and is now too big to ignore. As a part of an FMCG sales team, it is crucial to stay ahead of the curve and take advantage of this new trend before your competitors do. To prepare your e-commerce site for voice queries, there are four effective ways you can implement.

1. Optimize your content to increase your chances of appearing in voice searches.

2. Add a new skill to Google and Alexa voice assistant devices.

3. Offer voice-based navigation on your mobile app and website.

4. Ensure your products can be purchased with a simple flow using voice commands.

By implementing these strategies, you can prepare your e-commerce site for voice queries and stay ahead of the competition.

2. ARTIFICIAL REALITY (AR) AND ARTIFICIAL INTELLIGENCE (AI) WILL ENHANCE THE E-COMMERCE EXPERIENCE

Investing in AI and AR technologies has become a game-changer for online sellers, offering them a competitive edge and helping them stay ahead of the curve. According to estimates, online sellers spent $7.3 billion on AI in 2022 alone. This trend is expected to continue in the coming years as more and more businesses realize the potential of these advanced technologies. More than 120,000 stores already use AR technologies to offer customers a rich and immersive buying experience.

By leveraging AI, online sellers can provide personalized guidance and recommendations to their customers, making them feel valued and appreciated. AI analyzes shoppers' past purchase history and browsing behavior to show them products they are more likely to purchase, which helps to increase sales and customer satisfaction.

Unlike in physical stores, where customers can touch and feel the products they intend to buy, online shoppers cannot. This is where AR comes into play, as it helps eliminate this hurdle by letting customers see how a particular product would look on them even before they buy it. This not only helps to reduce the return rate but also enhances the overall shopping experience for customers.

By implementing AI and AR in your e-commerce store, you will see a significant increase in conversions and a decrease in the return rate. With AI and AR, you can create a seamless and personalized shopping experience that will help you stand out in the crowded e-commerce market and drive growth for your business.

3. EMERGENCE OF NEW PAYMENT METHODS

Accepting customers' preferred payment methods is crucial for the success of any e-commerce business. In today's digital age, digital wallets like Google Pay, Samsung Pay, Apple Pay, and PayPal are widely used alongside debit and credit cards. However, online shop owners can benefit significantly from accepting cryptocurrencies, especially Bitcoin, due to their low transaction fees and non-reversible transactions. By 2023, many e-commerce businesses will likely start accepting cryptocurrencies as a primary payment method.

4. MOBILE COMMERCE WILL DOMINATE E-COMMERCE

As online shopping gains more consumer trust, they are increasingly comfortable using their mobile devices to purchase. In fact, by the end of 2023, mobile devices are projected to account for almost 73% of all e-commerce sales. Moreover, a website that is not mobile-friendly can cause 30% of online shoppers to abandon their carts mid-purchase.

As an online seller, it is crucial to prioritize improving the customer experience for mobile users. Here are some practical ways to optimize your e-commerce site for mobile devices:

- Use the Google Mobile-Friendly Test[53] to evaluate your website's mobile-friendliness. This tool can identify loading issues and show whether your online store is responsive.

- Consider creating a Progressive Web App (PWA) for your store. PWAs are faster than websites, allowing customers to view previously browsed pages without internet access.

- Implement Accelerated Mobile Pages (AMP) for shoppers visiting your site on smartphones.

- Ensure your checkout process is seamless on mobile devices, and find ways to simplify it further.

- Manually test your mobile site to ensure easy navigation, product viewing, and zooming options.

---

53 https://search.google.com/test/mobile-friendly

By taking these steps, you can provide your customers with a satisfying mobile shopping experience.

KEY TAKEAWAY

Staying up-to-date with the latest e-commerce trends is crucial for businesses, especially those in the highly competitive FMCG market. As the e-commerce industry continues to grow at a rapid pace, it is imperative to not only keep yourself informed about the latest trends but also to implement them effectively. By doing so, you can boost your sales and advance your career.

REFERENCES

1. https://www.businessnewsdaily.com/7839-best-crm-software.html

2. https://pipeline.zoominfo.com/marketing/lead-scoring

3. https://blog.close.com/sales-commission-structure-for-startups

4. https://www.revenue.io/inside-sales-glossary/what-is-a-sales-stack

5. https://www.salesforce.com/

6. https://www.aviso.com/

7. https://www.dnb.com/products/marketing-sales/dnb-hoovers.html

8. https://www.inmotionnow.com/project-workflow/storytelling-coca-cola-marketing/

9. https://analytics.google.com/analytics/web/

10. https://www.quicksprout.com/consumer-psychology/

11. https://www.allego.com/blog/capturing-the-roi-of-sales-training/

12. https://salesinsightslab.com/sales-strategy-consultant/

13. https://salesengine.com/who-we-are/

14. https://brooksgroup.com/sales-training/impact-sales-team-training-program

15. https://clickup.com/

16. https://milestoneplanner.com/

17. https://powerbi.microsoft.com/en-us/

18. https://blog.bridgegroupinc.com/hubfs/resources/2017_
    SaaS_AE_Metrics.pdf?t=1525961943442

19. https://www.mckinsey.com/industries/high-
    tech/our-insights/the-social-economy

20. https://www.badgermapping.com/

21. https://www.gallup.com/cliftonstrengths/en/252137/home.aspx

22. https://www.tmbc.com/standout/

23. https://www.groovehq.com/customer-service-statistics

24. https://www.slideshare.net/RightNow/2011-
    customer-experience-impact-report

25. http://www.oracle.com/us/products/applications/commerce/
    live-help-on-demand/oracle-live-help-wp-aamf-1624138.pdf

26. https://www.forrester.com/report/The+US+Custom
    er+Experience+Index+Q1+2015/-/E-RES117482

27. https://www.hubspot.com/products/crm

28. https://www.hubspot.com/products/marketing/social-inbox

29. https://zoom.us/

30. https://powerbi.microsoft.com/en-us/blog/tag/office-365/

31. https://taskful.com/

32. https://culturedcode.com/things/

33. https://www.routexl.com/

34. https://batchgeo.com/

35. https://mapline.com/

36. https://www.megaventory.com/

37. https://www.zoho.com/inventory/

38. https://www.inflowinventory.com/

39. https://www.odoo.com/app/inventory

40. https://www.freshworks.com/crm/sales/

41. https://www.pipedrive.com/

42. https://www.salesforce.com/

43. https://www.indeed.com/career/sales-manager/salaries

44. https://www.bitrix24.com/

45. https://www.jobinterviewquestions.com/order-clerk/order-booker

46. https://www.investopedia.com/terms/m/marketsegmentation.asp

47. https://upboard.io/market-segmentation-online-tools-templates-software/

48. https://robyncambruzzi.com/portfolio/vitaminwater-hydration-station/

49. https://www.intelex.com/products/applications/

50. https://dbxtra.com/

51. https://pathmonk.com/lead-qualification-tool/

52. https://www.yotpo.com/

53. https://search.google.com/test/mobile-friendly

ABOUT THE AUTHOR

Manal Haddad's journey is a testament to the power of hard work and continuous learning. He is an accomplished business professional with extensive experience in sales, marketing, business development, and consulting. He has managed multinational organizations and international brands and has led cross-cultural teams to success. Today, Manal uses his knowledge and expertise to help business owners develop high-growth strategies and reach their goals. As a passionate mentor, he is committed to inspiring the next generation of leaders and empowering them with the knowledge and skills they need to impact the world positively. He believes in sharing knowledge to shape a better future. His writings reflect his enthusiasm and dedication to helping individuals pursue their entrepreneurial dreams. He is the author of several books on marketing, sales, distribution, process implementation, and leadership.

In his personal life, Manal is a devoted husband and father. He relishes listening to the freedom of expression in Jazz and feeling the thrill of cruising on his motorcycle on the open road in his free time. Visit him at www.manalhaddad.com.